The

Collie

An Owner's Guide To

A HAPPY HEALTHY PET

Howell Book House

IDG Books Worldwide, Inc.
An International Data Group Company
Foster City, CA • Chicago, IL • Indianapolis, IN • New York, NY • Southlake, TX

Howell Book House
IDG Books Worldwide, Inc.
An International Data Group Company
919 E. Hillsdale Boulevard
Suite 400
Foster City, CA 94404

For general information on IDG Books Worldwide's books in the U.S., please call our
Consumer Customer Service department at 800-762-2974. For reseller information,
including discounts and premium sales, please call our Reseller Customer Service
department at 800-434-3422.

Library of Congress Cataloging-in-Publication Data
The collie.
    p.cm—(A Owner's guide to a happy healthy pet)
  Includes bibliographical references (p.).
  ISBN 1-58245-008-0
   1. Collie. I. Howell Book House. II. Series.

SF429.C6C56 1999
636.737'4—dc21

Manufactured in the United States of America
10 9 8 7 6 5 4 3 2 1

Series Director: Amanda Pisani
Book Design: Michele Laseau
Cover Design: Iris Jeromnimon
Illustration: Laura Robbins
Photography: All photography by Mary Bloom unless otherwise noted.
            Front cover, inset and back cover photos by Mary Bloom.
Production Team: Heather Pope, Carol Sheehan, Julie Tripetti

Contents

Welcome
to the
World

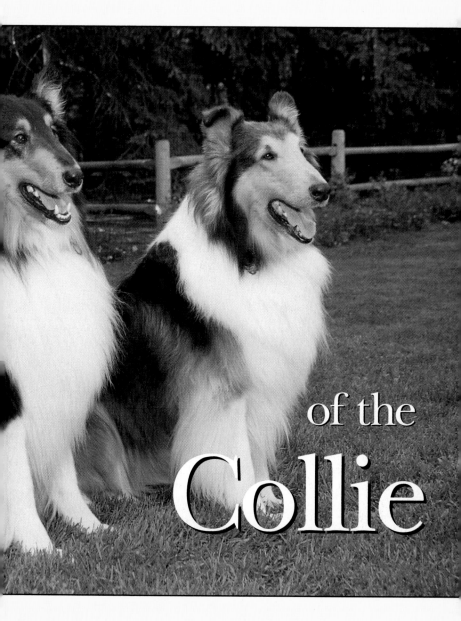

of the
Collie

External Features of the Collie

chapter 1

What Is a Collie?

To know what a Collie is, just ask a child. Generations of children have grown up reading Albert Payson Terhune's wonderful Collie stories, Eric Knight's *Lassie Come Home*, and seeing "Lassie" in the movies or on TV, tirelessly coming to the rescue, time and again. No breed has even come close in capturing public affection and imagination.

Wherever we take our Collies, someone always stops us with a wonderful story of the Collie they owned. We find the "Collies in fiction" are matched and even exceeded by the true exploits of real Collies everywhere.

Collies are the caretakers of their world, and nothing is so small it escapes their notice. They were developed as hardy, intelligent herding dogs by self-sufficient inhabitants of isolated communities in Scotland and other parts of the British Isles. They were more than stock dogs, they were partners, for their human family's very survival depended on them. Those first Collies were bred to have almost human intelligence and reasoning ability; to be gentle, loving and loyal; and to staunchly defend those they loved. Happily, they have passed this legacy to the Collies that brighten peoples' lives today.

In many ways, the Collie is the ideal family dog and enjoys a place in many hearts the world over.

Collies have won the national *Dog Hero of the Year* award more often than any other breed. With Queen Victoria's patronage, the Collie caught the attention of a dedicated group of breeders in England who determined to make this breed as beautiful on the outside as on the inside. That they succeeded is a happy historical fact.

The Breed Standard

All recognized dog breeds have a standard that serves as a description of the ideal dog. No one dog will meet every quality in the standard, but the goal of breeders is to produce dogs that bear that standard's characteristics.

The following excerpts from the official American Kennel Club standard for the Collie appear in italic type. Because of the length and technical nature of the standard, only the most important sections have been excerpted.

GENERAL CHARACTER

The standard begins with a first impression: *The Collie is a lithe, strong, responsive, active dog carrying no useless timber, standing naturally straight and firm. The deep, moderately wide chest shows strength, the sloping shoulders and well-bent hocks indicate speed and grace, and the face shows high intelligence. The Collie presents an impressive, proud picture of true balance . . .*

The standard draws a mental picture of a proud dog—graceful, balanced and strong. You can almost see him standing on a hillside watching his flocks, his beautiful head high and alert, his body ready to move at a moment's notice. For all the technical explanations necessary to describe in detail all that goes into the making of this proud, beautiful animal, you now have in your mind's eye the picture that is "Collie."

WHAT IS A BREED STANDARD?

A breed standard—a detailed description of an individual breed—is meant to portray the ideal specimen of that breed. This includes ideal structure, temperament, gait, type—all aspects of the dog. Because the standard describes an ideal specimen, it isn't based on any particular dog. It is a concept against which judges compare actual dogs and breeders strive to produce dogs. At a dog show, the dog that wins is the one that comes closest, in the judge's opinion, to the standard for its breed. Breed standards are written by the breed parent clubs, the national organizations formed to oversee the well-being of the breed. They are voted on and approved by the members of the parent clubs.

HEAD

The Collie's head and expression set him apart from other breeds. The head is described as *inclined to lightness . . . A heavy-headed dog lacks the necessary bright, alert, full of sense look that contributes so greatly to expression. Both in front and profile view the head bears a general resemblance to a well-blunted lean wedge, being smooth and clean in outline and nicely balanced in proportion . . . A midpoint between the inside corners of the eyes (which is the center of a correctly placed stop) is the center of balance in length* of head. *The teeth are of good size, meeting in a scissors bite. Overshot or undershot jaws are undesirable, the latter being more severely penalized.* In a scissors bite, the upper incisors overlap just outside and in front of the lower incisors. When the upper incisors extend beyond the lowers, the dog is "overshot"; when the lower incisors extend beyond the upper ones, the dog is "undershot." It is common for young adolescents to be slightly overshot as the head lengthens, but they outgrow it, and a very slight overshot is not considered a serious fault. More extensive overshot bites give a chinless or weak appearance. An undershot bite is foreign to the breed, distorting the shape of the head and giving it a "Roman"(concave) profile. Undershot and severe overshot bites often cause eating, alignment and dentition problems.

The Collie is a proud dog— graceful, balanced and strong.

EYES

Because of the combination of the flat skull, the arched eyebrows, the slight stop and the rounded muzzle, the foreface must be chiseled to form a receptacle for the eyes and they are necessarily placed obliquely to give them the required forward outlook . . . They are almond-shaped, of medium size and never properly appear to be large or prominent . . . The eyes have a clear, bright appearance, expressing intelligent inquisitiveness, particularly when the ears are drawn up and the dog is on the alert . . . A large, round, full eye seriously detracts from the desired "sweet" expression. Perhaps the eyes make the most lasting impression, for they are the very soul of the breed. The Collie's expression is soft, sweet and enchanting. You seem unable to pull away as you gaze at this lovely face, nor can you resist smiling back. It is the very unique combination of head parts that produces this charming effect. Other breed standards also call for an almond-shaped eye, or even an obliquely set eye, but they still do not produce the picture that is uniquely "Collie."

Because of the length and shape of the Collie's skull and the chiseling effect necessary to set the eyes properly in the skull, the almond-shaped eye not only slants upward but to the side. Perhaps no other feature so sets the Collie apart from other breeds or leaves such a lasting impression.

The distinctive Collie's ears contribute to his soft expression.

EARS

When in repose the ears are folded lengthwise and thrown back into the frill. On the alert they are drawn well up on the backskull and are carried about three-quarters erect, with about one-fourth of the ear tipping or "breaking" forward. A dog with prick ears or low ears cannot show true expression. The ears set off the expression, the alert, slightly tipped shape aiding the softness of expression.

BODY AND LEGS

The body is described as firm, hard and muscular, a trifle long in proportion to height, with straight, muscular forelegs and sinewy hind legs, muscular at the thighs. The hocks and stifles are well bent. This refers to the angles in the conformation of the rear leg; when there is sufficient angulation (bend) the dog will move with a stronger backward push with more reach, giving more flexibility, speed and smoothness.

GAIT

The beautiful, flowing gait is characteristic of the breed. Remember our first impression?—*The Collie is a lithe, strong, responsive, active dog . . .* Lithe means flexible, supple, agile, and the Collie in action makes a breathtaking picture, seeming to barely touch the ground, with a long, reaching stride.

At the trot, the Collie characteristically "single tracks." Viewed from the front or back at a trot, the legs appear to converge toward the midline of the body, the center of balance. This is nature's means of conserving energy; it keeps the feet under the dog's center of gravity. The faster they go, the closer the feet will appear to fall in a straight line. Dogs that do not single track will show a choppy, rolling or pacing gait.

Watch a Collie herding sheep and you can appreciate the breed's beautiful, flowing gait. Here the Rough tricolor Daydreams Millknock Knockout, HT, PT, CGC and co-owner Jim Smotrel keep the stock moving.

Single tracking allows the balance and center of gravity to work for and with the dog, he is always ready to shift direction, is never off balance, is collected and in control. *Viewed from the side the reasonably long, "reaching" stride is smooth and even, keeping the back line firm and level.* The Collie moves with grace and ease, seeming almost to float while barely touching the ground. He should not bounce or roll, but should cover ground effortlessly.

TAIL

The Collie's long, proud tail finishes the picture, *carried low when the dog is quiet, the end having an upward* twist or "swirl." When the Collie is gaiting, however, it is carried gaily, but never over the back.

COAT

Collies have two coat varieties and four recognized colors, with a wide variation of acceptable white markings.

Although Lassie has popularized the sable and white color and the rough coat, there is enough selection to satisfy anyone's taste. While the glorious coat of the Rough Collie is his crowning glory, in today's wash-and-wear world the Smooth Collie is gaining popularity with his sleek beauty and easy-care coat.

Both varieties are double-coated, with a dense, soft undercoat that repels water and protects against heat and cold. The Smooth variety has a short, dense, hard, flat outer coat of good texture, with an abundance of undercoat. The longer hair of the Rough variety is well fitting, and abundant except on the head and legs. The outer coat is straight and harsh to the touch. The undercoat is soft, furry and thick.

The Rough Collie carries a huge mane and frill. The face is smooth, the forelegs are smooth but well feathered and the hind legs are smooth below the hocks. The tail and hips are profusely coated. The coat is never to be so profuse as to hide the dog's outline and lose overall balance.

The Smooth Collie, Ch. Reignmaker's Great Scott, owned by the author, is from a family of service dogs.

COLOR

The four recognized colors are "Sable and White," "Tri-color," "Blue Merle" and "White." There is no preference among them. The "Sable and White" is predominantly sable (a fawn

11

sable color of varying shades from light gold to dark mahogany) with white markings usually on the chest, neck, legs, feet and the tip of the tail. A blaze may appear on the foreface or backskull or both. The "Tri-color" is predominantly black, carrying white markings as in a "Sable and White" and has tan shadings on and about the head and legs. The "Blue Merle" is a mottled or "marbled" color predominantly blue-grey and black with white markings as in the "Sable and White" and usually has tan shadings as in the "Tri-color." The "White" is predominantly white, preferably with sable, tri-color or blue merle markings.

THE AMERICAN KENNEL CLUB

Familiarly referred to as "the AKC," the American Kennel Club is a nonprofit organization devoted to the advancement of purebred dogs. The AKC maintains a registry of recognized breeds and adopts and enforces rules for dog events including shows, obedience trials, field trials, hunting tests, lure coursing, herding, earthdog trials, agility and the Canine Good Citizen program. It is a club of clubs, established in 1884 and composed, today, of over 500 autonomous dog clubs throughout the United States. Each club is represented by a delegate; the delegates make up the legislative body of the AKC, voting on rules and electing directors. The American Kennel Club maintains the Stud Book, the record of every dog ever registered with the AKC, and publishes a variety of materials on purebred dogs, including a monthly magazine, books and numerous educational pamphlets. For more information, contact the AKC at the address listed in Chapter 13, "Resources," and look for the names of their publications in Chapter 12, "Recommended Reading."

A century ago, Collies appeared in numerous colors, the most common being black and tan, but including blue or red merle, sable, red or tan, with or without white, and black and white, a color now lost to the breed. Old Smooth lines brought in a slate blue with no merling, still seen at times. The absence of white markings was a prized feature, in the erroneous belief that the lack of white denoted purity of breeding.

The tricolor phase is black with tan points over the eyes; tan along the cheeks, chest, legs and tail; and normal white markings. The black should be a rich, jet-black, almost blue-black; the white should be sparkling; and the tan rich, all producing an eye-catching combination. Black and tan, with or without white markings, is as old as the breed itself. White markings have been a distinctive part of the breed for most of its modern history.

In the late 1800s, blue merle coloring was very common among working sheepdogs. When breeders began breeding for the showring, sable was scarce but rapidly became the color of choice. A Rough Blue Merle Collie Club was founded in 1907, and this unique color was saved from oblivion. Blue merle Collies are greatly admired today. This is an exquisite combination of silvery-blue, marbled with black, the usual white markings, and rich tan points as in the tricolor. Sometimes one or both eyes will be all or partially merle or china (blue or white) in color; there is no specific penalty, although dark brown eyes are preferred. The clearer and more silvery the blue, the more breathtaking the dog.

When a blue merle is bred to a sable, some offspring will be silvery-shaded sables. Called "sable merles," they range from an almost lemony color to deep orange, usually with darker sable marbling and gray-tipped ears. Sable merles draw strong feelings among Collie breeders, primarily because one or both eyes may be blue. The standard calls for eyes to be dark-colored and, except for blue merles, to be matched. Many feel that the startling look of blue eyes in a sable face detracts from the sweet Collie expression. Others are tantalized by the unique look, and except for the demands of the showring, it is a personal choice.

The Collie is one of the breeds in which the blue merle color phase is found.

The white Collie is a "color-bred" white. Selective breeding has produced a spectacular Collie that is 90 percent white, with a fully colored head (sable, tricolor or blue merle, with or without a blaze) and that may have one or more colored body markings. White Collies came into fashion as the favorites of Queen Victoria's children, and became status symbols with British and French aristocracy. The rage for whites reached America, where they were developed and remain today an integral part of the Collie breed. Unfortunately, white fell into disfavor in Great Britain and elsewhere, with their standards severely penalizing the color. Today, white popularity is increasing around the world and much of the breeding stock is being imported from America. The favorites of Queens and Presidents, it seems only proper that whites regain their place of favor.

The white color phase is the least familiar of all Collie colors, though it can be as attractive as all the others.

In early Collie history, too, predominantly all-white herding dogs were used as stock guardians, as they could mingle with and appear to be a part of the flock, to catch both animal and human predators by surprise. The strong natural guarding instincts of the white Collie were channeled into this protective role. They were raised with the sheep, who learned to trust and follow them. As livestock farming methods changed, the need for guardian dogs was replaced by a need for driving, gathering and herding dogs. The white dogs, being less intimidating to the sheep, were less useful for these chores and their need diminished.

SIZE

Dogs are from 24 to 26 inches at the shoulder and weigh from 60 to 75 pounds. Bitches are from 22 to 24 inches at the shoulder, weighing from 50 to 65 pounds. An undersize or an oversize Collie is penalized according to the extent to which the dog appears to be undersize or oversize. Although the height and weight of Collies may vary considerably, it is important always that the dog be balanced, agile and never appear cumbersome or awkward.

EXPRESSION

Expression is one of the most important points in considering the relative value of Collies. Expression, like the term "character" is difficult to define in words. It is not a fixed point as in color, weight or height, and it is something the uninitiated can properly understand only by optical illustration. In general, however, it may be said to be the combined product of the shape and balance of the skull and muzzle, the placement, size, shape and color of the eye and the position, size and carriage of the ears . . . The Collie cannot be judged properly until its expression has been carefully evaluated.

Without proper expression, even given everything else, a dog would still not be a proper Collie. Throughout, the standard stresses that intelligence is a key characteristic, but since it cannot be measured in the showring, you can only hope to "see" it some other way. Words like "face shows high intelligence" and "expressing intelligent inquisitiveness" direct the observer to the expression.

chapter 2

The
Collie's
Ancestry

The Collie's history is a part of British heritage. The transformation of this hardworking herding dog into the glamorous Collie of today is well documented; however, much of its earlier history has been lost or romanticized.

Rough and Smooth coat varieties appear to have developed from the same root stock at about the same time in different parts of Britain and for a variety of purposes. They were eventually combined into two varieties of the same breed by judicious interbreeding and selection, and in the late 1800s a combined Rough and Smooth Breed standard was issued in Britain. The American Kennel Club registers all Collies as one breed.

The Early Rough Collie

The political and social structure of the Picts, Scots and Britons of early times were much alike, based on tribal kingdoms, with small homesteads belonging to a related group, surrounded by land used mostly as pasture for their flocks. For centuries, migrant farmers in Ireland and Scotland maintained versatile herding dogs as guards, to carry messages, guard livestock from predators and circle the herds to protect them. Obviously, these dogs were essential to their masters' very survival. These people spoke a common dialect from which the name "Collie," meaning "useful," was derived.

Bred pure for centuries on remote farms, the early Collies already had longer, finer heads than other working sheepdogs, and the softer expression that would later characterize the breed.

This 1896 study by Maud Earl, famous 19th-century animal artist, depicts a typical Collie of the time.

During the Roman occupation, wool was essential, and selective breeding developed a split into two types of herding dogs, the all-around versatile stock dog (Rough Collie) and the specialized sheepdog, from a common root source.

The Early Smooth Collie

The Romans had large, shorthaired "circling" dogs to protect and drive the flocks, which, when crossed with the native herding dogs, were probably ancestors of the Smooth Collie. The early Rough Collie, developed primarily in the Scottish Highlands, was generally longhaired, smaller than the contemporary version and lower on leg. The Smooth looked more like our modern Collie, taller, leaner and more elegant than the Roughs of that time. These dogs were utilized primarily in northern England as both herders and drovers.

These Smooth-coated dogs were noted for their intelligence, even temperaments, loyalty, endurance and stamina. Each dog had a specific task; some leading, some keeping the stock together and moving and some circling and guarding.

Present-day Smooth Collies resemble their ancestors more than do present-day Roughs.

Changing Times— The 1800s

The Industrial Revolution and the coming of the railroad to Britain brought town and country closer together, with city people attending rural events, where they got their first glimpse of the Collie. The nurturing instinct that made her so useful with livestock also made her an ideal children's companion, and her natural protective instincts, honed over generations, made her a perfect protector of home and family.

The versatile herding dogs soon found other work to do. They accompanied the butcher on his daily rounds, guarding the contents of the delivery wagon from thieves while he stopped to make deliveries. The more elegant and easily kept Smooth Collies were used to dress up the butcher's entry for the "trade turnout," a form of competition that was the highlight of early agricultural shows. This started a fashion in carriage dogs, and in the 1800s the Smooth Collie, not the Dalmatian, was the fashionable ladies' carriage dog.

During this time, the romantic image of the kilted Scotsman and his faithful Collie caught the imagination of artists and poets. Scotland's most famous poet, Robert Burns, wrote of his faithful dog, Luath, ". . . a ploughman's Collie." "He was a gash (wise) and faithfu' type . . . His honest, sonsie (comely), baws'nt face (a white blaze, showing great intelligence), ay gat him friends in ilka (every) place . . . His breast was white, his tousie (back), weel clad (well covered) wi' coat o' glossy black; His gawsie (jolly) tail, wi' upward curl, Hung owre (over) his hurdies (hips) wi' a swirl."

Soon royalty would take an interest in the Collie, and from that point, its popularity grew rapidly. Queen Victoria, fascinated with Scotland and a dog lover in general, purchased Balmoral Castle and established a kennel of Scottish breeds, including both Rough and Smooth Collies. The Queen was a great admirer of Collies, often watching her shepherds working with their dogs at Balmoral, and attended numerous shows and sheepdog trials. Victoria's constant companion for over fifteen years was a Smooth Collie named "Sharp," born in 1864. Upon his death, she erected a statue to him in Windsor Home Park, which can still be seen today.

One Breed, Two Varieties

Although there had always been crosses between the two varieties, by the Victorian era Collies were generally thought of as two breeds.

WHERE DID DOGS COME FROM?

It can be argued that dogs were right there at man's side from the beginning of time. As soon as human beings began to document their existence, the dog was among their drawings and inscriptions. Dogs were not just friends, they served a purpose: There were dogs to hunt birds, pull sleds, herd sheep, burrow after rats—even sit in laps! What your dog was originally bred to do influences the way it behaves. The American Kennel Club recognizes over 140 breeds, and there are hundreds more distinct breeds around the world. To make sense of the breeds, they are grouped according to their size or function. The AKC has seven groups:

1) Sporting, 2) Working, 3) Herding, 4) Hounds, 5) Terriers, 6) Toys, 7) Nonsporting

Can you name a breed from each group? Here's some help: (1) Golden Retriever; (2) Doberman Pinscher; (3) Collie; (4) Beagle; (5) Scottish Terrier; (6) Maltese; (7) Dalmatian. All modern domestic dogs (Canis familiaris) are related, however different they look, and are all descended from Canis lupus, the gray wolf.

When it became apparent that these two Collies, so different in appearance, were by nature and breeding very similar, breeders began crossing the varieties to obtain the best of both. By 1870, crossbreeding was routine, with Smooths and Roughs appearing in the same litter. However, another effect of this cross benefited both varieties. The formerly shorter legged, longer bodied Rough with forward-thrusting neck and the taller, leaner, more elegant Smooth combined to produce the beautiful beginnings of the modern Collie.

Royal favor played a major part in the Collie's meteoric rise from shepherd's dog to one of the world's favorite companions.

The Collie as Show Dog

The first formal all-breed dog show anywhere was held in Birmingham, England, in December 1860, with 267 entries for twenty-five breeds, including five Collies (although combined in a generic class for "Scotch sheepdogs"). Two years later, "Scotch Colleys" had their own class. The first separate classes for Smooth Coated Sheepdogs or Collies was in London in 1870, with two entries.

The Collie Comes to America

In 1879, the first Rough Collie was imported from England to America. J. P. Morgan and John D. Rockefeller, two of America's wealthiest men, vied to purchase England's very best Rough Collies, and the British breeders got in on a good thing. In 1900, 675 Collies were registered in America, compared to 265 ten years earlier, and 1 Collie finished its championship. By 1920, importation peaked and began to subside as American breeders evolved their own beautiful Collies. Two dogs, both born in England in 1912, Ch. Laund Limit and Ch. Magnet, would form the foundation for America's dominant sire line through their descendant, Ch. Alstead Eden Emerald, to whom the majority of top winning and producing

Rough Collies both in America and England can be directly traced.

The earliest record of Smooths being shown in the U.S. is at the 1888 Westminster Kennel Club show, with five entries. By 1890, Roughs and Smooths almost always competed together. However, because of the overwhelming popularity of the Rough variety, interest in the Smooth declined and the variety became all but extinct.

Margaret Haserot of Pebble Ledge Farm almost single-handedly revitalized Smooths in the U.S., producing the first Smooth champion in thirty-eight years, Ch. Pebble Ledge Bambi. Bambi's children laid the foundation for modern Smooths in America. Margaret was determined to continue, alone if necessary, when the American Smooth Collie Association, Inc. was formed in 1957 and the Smooth Collie was off and running again in America.

Ch. Black Hawk of Kasan ushered in a new era for Smooths and changed Collie history forever, breaking one record after ano-

The Smooth Collie's ease of care has made this variety increasingly popular as a pet and working dog.

ther, going Best of Breed at the Collie Club of America Specialty, a record only recently matched. He sired seventy-five champions and is in the pedigree of numerous winners and producers in both varieties. Hawk brought the Smooth Collie to the attention of the Collie world, and interest in this variety continues to grow.

English imports dominated the American show scene until the late 1930s, when World War II stopped the ready availability of imported dogs. American breeders had to rely on themselves, and so began the development of the American Collie and the uniquely American breeder.

Livestock Workers, Then and Now

In 1876 in England, the Kennel Club organized a sheepdog trial for pedigreed show Collies that became a disaster never repeated. Many people of that time and since have used that one example to prove that the brains were bred out of show Collies. No one stopped to think that neither the dogs nor the owners had probably ever seen stock before and had no idea what to do.

Interestingly, at around the same time, many show Collies were performing quite well at stock dog trials. Sheepdog trials were held in conjunction with the Dublin show from 1888, and Belfast held its first sheepdog trial in 1898, and a number of show Collies took part in both.

Today, Collies are again competing in herding events as owners return to the breed's roots and the joy of a working companion. Collies today return to their old occupation as if they had never left it, just another job to be done.

The Smooth Collie has shown herself to be a highly capable and valued guide dog.

Collies as Guide and Service Dogs

I have been privileged to be uniquely involved with Collies as guide dogs for the blind. In 1949, a Rough tricolor, Prince, became the first purebred Collie guide dog. Hellen Tullis, his blind mistress, went from being a virtual shut-in to an award-winning lecturer and TV personality. Together they handled hundreds of national speaking engagements, and for three years Hellen produced and hosted a weekly TV program called, *As You Can See*. Hellen won *McCall's* magazine's award for Outstanding Woman in Radio and Television working in the public interest.

I began working with Dr. Lee Ford when she established her Shamrock Collie Research Laboratory in the mid-1950s. Hellen's remark that Prince was perfect in every way except for the long hair encouraged Dr. Ford's interest in the Smooth Collie as a guide dog, and by 1956 Lee was working with Leader Dogs for the Blind with her "Companion Collies for the Blind." Lee's first litter bred specifically for careers as guide dogs produced eight graduates, the first Smooth Collie guide dogs in the U.S. and possibly the world! I lost touch with Lee and the guide dog program several years later.

The development and use of service dogs is a relatively recent development. This is "Sir Austin," a well-known ambassador for the work with his owner, Jean Levitt.

However, in the mid-1980s a friend called to tell me a new guide dog school had just opened in Florida where I live—Southeastern Guide Dogs in Bradenton. I called to see if they might be interested in using any of our Smooth Collies, and the director agreed to meet with us and some of the dogs. After a visit to the school, we were totally dedicated to this wonderful project. When our expected litter didn't arrive, our daughter Katie made the biggest decision of all, and offered to let the school take Lancer, her own personal dog, because she knew if any dog could do it, he could. Lancer became practically a legend in his own time as he and his blind mistress, Donna Pass, became overnight celebrities in their small town.

When Donna enrolled at the University of Florida, Lancer was there to get her across campus and to class, and to help her make friends. The producers of a dinner theater production of *Little Orphan Annie* asked to use Lancer as Sandy, with Donna playing a cast member so she could be on stage with him. Lancer was a standout as Sandy, playing to standing ovations, but willingly returning to the harness and his beloved Donna when the play ended each day.

I met Hellen Tullis at a school function after she moved to Florida and was receiving a younger brother of Lancer as her guide dog. She cried as she told me about her wonderful Prince, and that the Collie people had listened to her and produced a "shorthaired" Collie. She will never know how much of a part she played in fostering interest in the Smooth Collie. Prince died in her arms after pushing her from the path of a truck, which hit him. The ambulance driver wouldn't allow Prince on board, so Hellen refused to leave him, cradling him in her arms while he died. After that tragic day, such discriminating practices have been outlawed.

Heroism comes naturally to Collies, and the stories of their lifesaving exploits are numerous and inspiring.

Collies Serve in Many Areas

Collies served in both World Wars, where they were used as sentries and messengers, prized for their intelligence, courage and loyalty. They are also used world-wide for search and rescue and in drug or explosives detection.

Collies, protective by their very nature, continue to win awards for heroism, always seeming to know what to do and how to do it, whether it is pushing someone out of traffic, or warning of a fire or a break-in, or protecting from danger. Collies perform their modern duties with the same dedication once given to herding. Obviously, Collies are marching in the modern world with their heads high and their eyes alight, able to handle every new challenge.

Famous Collies and Famous Owners

As the Collie was gaining in popularity in the U.S. as a show dog, he was also becoming America's darling as a family pet. Albert Payson Terhune established a legacy for his Sunnybank Collies through his marvelous books published in the 1920s and 1930s. Eric Knight wrote *Lassie Come Home* in 1940, which inspired eight movies and a TV series still in reruns. Metro-Goldwyn-Mayer made *Lassie Come Home* into a movie, starring Elizabeth Taylor, Roddy McDowell and a young sable and white Collie named "Pal," trained by Rudd Weatherwax. "Lassie" in the book was a tricolor, but Pal would forever set the sable color as the only Collie color in the minds of movie and TV viewers.

In a scene where the Collie had to swim a fast-moving river, Pal was taken to the middle of the river in a boat, dumped over the side and told to swim for shore. On reaching the shore, he took a few faltering steps and collapsed as if he had swum the whole river, giving the performance of his life. The director told Weatherwax that Pal might have gone into the river, but "Lassie" had come out, and Pal's career had begun.

Collies have been the devoted companions of the famous and everyday folks alike. All a Collie wants in return is love.

Many more films were made, and in 1954 the TV series began that would span two decades with 589 original episodes starring four generations of his descendants. That was just the beginning of a dynasty Rudd Weatherwax's son continues with Howard, Pal's eighth-generation descendant.

Many celebrities have been happy Collie owners, from Liz Taylor to Elvis Presley to country singer Mark Collie. Singer Jose Feliciano sang the National Anthem with his Smooth Collie guide dog at his side. Nell Carter, singer and TV star, has Collies. At least two U.S. Presidents had Collies: Calvin Coolidge and Lyndon B. Johnson. Collies love everyone.

FAMOUS OWNERS OF THE COLLIE

Nell Carter

Calvin Coolidge

Jose Feliciano

Lyndon B. Johnson

Elvis Presley

Elizabeth Taylor

Texas A&M's Collie mascot is named Reveille; in fact, the school now has mascot #6 since some cadets found a Collie in 1931 and attempted to hide it. The Collie began howling at dawn, so gaining her name, and there has been a Collie there ever since. As each retires, a new puppy takes her place. The remains of four previous Reveilles are in a special graveyard outside the football stadium where they are buried with their paws and faces pointed so they can see the scoreboard, "so they can always watch the Aggies outscore their opponents on the field," according to the student handbook. A marker at the gravesites proclaims Reveille as "First Lady of A&M." She is the highest ranking member of the cadets and is addressed by freshmen cadets as "Miss Reveille, ma'am." She wears five diamonds stitched onto the maroon and white blanket draped over her back, like a five-star general. Other than guide dogs, Reveille is the only animal allowed in all buildings on campus and attends classes with the mascot corporal, who must take the Collie wherever he goes, even on dates. When a Reveille dies, she gets a military funeral, complete with a twenty-one-gun salute.

chapter 3

The World According to the Collie

To his friends, a Collie is a joy to live with. There is no better family dog; his loyalty, bravery and almost human intelligence is legendary. However, developing these traits requires loving, attentive care from his human family.

Intelligent and active, Collies can quickly become bored, and a bored Collie, left to his own devices, will find ways to entertain himself. Sometimes these diversions can be very destructive. When you plan to include a Collie in your world, plan ahead and you will have a truly splendid companion for his entire lifetime.

The Vigilant Guardian

Collies are not demanding—they want to please, but not submissively. They study their surroundings and try to fit in. Collies are very voice-oriented, in tune to your facial expressions and body language. Notoriously easy to train, to housetrain and pick up your home routine in a snap, a Collie makes a great watchdog and will always alert you to strange noises or unfamiliar people. True to the primal herding legacy, the breed is very protective, and your Collie will subtly place himself between you and any perceived danger. He will take hold of your hand and lead you where he wants you to go, or bark to get you to follow him. Trust your gut instinct if your Collie seems to be trying to "tell you something"—he probably is.

I grew up with a Lassie look-alike, who protected me from neighborhood bullies, sat with me endlessly while I read to him and was truly my very best friend. "Sandy" gave me an enduring love for Collies.

My own children learned to walk hanging on to a gentle Collie. Later in this chapter are stories of their own rescues and relationships with our Collies.

The Collie's strong nurturing instinct results from his herding background. His devotion to his family and an uncanny ability to almost read minds stems from his early role as the companion to the shepherd and his family, a role in which he was considered a working partner and equal.

Collies instinctively assume responsibility for the entire household. He knows when to get everyone up for work and school, when to watch for the school bus and when to pace worriedly when someone is late getting home. He understands getting up early five days a week and sleeping later on weekends. Collies want to know where everyone is and will unobtrusively follow family members about the house. If there are several

---

CHARACTERISTICS OF A COLLIE

Intelligent

Intuitive

Fun-Loving

Easily trained

Alert

Protective

Sensitive

---

people, he will routinely check on each. He will attempt to gather the playing children into a group he can watch over.

The previous chapter mentions our work with guide dogs. These dogs must use "intelligent disobedience" because they are often the only barrier between their sight-impaired masters and harm. Collies thrive in this role, just as they do with children, and work with a sparkle in their eyes and wagging tails. Collies always seem to sense what to do.

When the guide dog school we work with was trying to match an elderly lady with a guide dog, all the available dogs seemed to overwhelm the rather fragile lady. A young Collie was brought from the kennel as a last resort. He had not yet finished training and, typical of any enthusiastic young dog, he was rather rambunctious. Once in harness and paired with the lady, this Collie instinctively became very calm, taking small steps and matching his demeanor to the needs of his new partner. He gladly took on this new role to the delight of his blind mistress and all observers.

A Collie makes an ideal companion for a loving owner of any age.

Collies have a unique ability to reason things out when there is no one to guide them. Erik, one of the guide dogs we bred, was leading his blind master down an unfamiliar street in a large city when the man became disoriented. After several false attempts, he knew he needed help, but there was no one around. He tried to keep from panicking but did not know how to tell Erik how to take him to safety. Finally, in desperation, he told Erik to "Take me home." Now, Erik did not have any idea how to get home from this unfamiliar place, but he did remember how they got there in the first place. He took his master to the bus stop where they had started out! From there it was smooth sailing.

The Adaptive Collie

A Collie can be sedate and dignified inside the home, enthusiastic outside at play or an entertaining companion for a quiet walk. Collies love life and everything in it, and seem to know when to turn their normal responses on and off. We have worked stock with our Collies for long hours; they approach the activity with enthusiasm and dedication. At other times, they lounge around the house contentedly or help the kids watch TV! Collies make up their own complicated and very structured games with people, other dogs or other pets in the home. Your Collie will bring in a baby squirrel or bird and seem to say, "Fix it please," as he delivers it unhurt, watching seriously as you work with it. Our home was always full of kids and pets and wild animals being restored to health, and the Collies were an integral part of this.

Our Own Experiences

Collies adore games, and will play anything the children want with equal enthusiasm. They easily grasp the game rules, and will even make up their own very involved rules when playing together. When our children were quite young, we had moved onto eighty rural acres, so we were pretty isolated. My son had started school and would often bring friends home afterwards to play. One afternoon, one of the boys' mothers was visiting, and after I had introduced her to my son and his little sister, she kept looking around. I asked what was wrong and she said she had especially wanted to meet my other son as all the kids were raving about how much fun he was to play with. I hesitated and explained I had no other son. She said she was sure she was right, his name was "Douglas." With that I laughed and called out "Douglas"; our big tricolor Collie ran to me, watching intently to see if the adults were going to join in his game with the kids. The children considered Douglas a pal and an equal. They never thought to explain that he was a dog.

Collies and children are a natural combination. The breed also gets along happily with other family pets.

The Collie's proverbial heroism, mentioned earlier, is part of the author's family history. This dog, so gentle and understanding, can become a staunch protector instantly. We once had eight Quarter Horses on our acreage, cross fenced away from the house and the yard where the children played. One morning from inside the house, I could hear the thundering sound of running hooves. I was able to watch my 6-year-old son and 2-year-old daughter out the window as they played. The horses had broken through the far pasture fence and were racing across the field toward the house. They were racing each other and had no idea where they were going, but the children were right in their path. I screamed to my son to grab his sister, yelled for Douglas and flew to the door at the other end of the house. In that split second, Douglas had turned seven of the eight horses. My son had grabbed his sister and climbed into the yard swing. The remaining horse trotted into the yard, calmer now, and trotted on. A brave boy and an equally courageous Collie had turned what could have been a tragedy into just another family story.

Collies will use only the force necessary to handle a situation, considering it their role in life. Whether stopping one of the kids from running in front of a car, or moving a baby back from the water, or challenging an intruder, they seem to know just what to do. In play, my husband was once pretending to hit my son with a stick. Ryan, one of our Collies, was watching intently. My son was screaming, "Don't hit me!" but was giggling; his sister and I were laughing. It was obvious no one was in danger, but still Ryan knew it was his duty to protect the children. He came forward, confiscated the stick and carried it into another room, returning with a big grin and a wagging tail! He had simply handled the situation!

My daughter was in her room one day after school when Nachos, her Collie, kept running in, barking insistently and demanding she follow

Collies have the well-developed ability to reason out situations and invent their own games.

her. My daughter finally gave in and went with her, only to find that bad wiring in an old kitchen range had started a fire that was spreading to the kitchen cabinets. The fire was extinguished safely thanks to a Collie who wouldn't take "no" for an answer.

Our Collies didn't want the kids to climb trees or put their heads underwater when swimming. They would block the children back from what they saw as danger or put themselves between a stranger and myself or the children, appearing to just happen to be there; or stand just behind the stranger, unseen but in charge. Collies can and will bite if the situation warrants it, but they are sensible and are very capable of analyzing what force, if any, is needed.

Children raised with Collies share a lasting bond and have a deep appreciation for their furry friends. Patrick was called in to drive the gremlins from under the bed, or listen to a strange noise outside the window, and his furry warmth provided a big safety net in my daughter's life. When she began dating, she would always tell her dates they needed Patrick's approval. Patrick was, to their surprise, not her big brother or her stepfather, but the Collie checking them out with such intensity.

Challenges Posed by Collies

Sometimes the very things that make a Collie so right for one family will make it all wrong for another. While we always appreciated and trusted Collies' judgment, other people may want a dog more inclined to instant obedience. Collies are well-behaved in the home, rather laid-back, and we usually just tell them to "lie down" if we want them out of the way. They wander off to a comfortable space and snooze until something entertaining interests them, or someone moves.

Collies are willingly obedience-trained, but the trainer must be sure to be lavish in praise.

DON'T TRAIN TOO HARD!

A Collie can be trained to instant obedience, but the trainer must know how to do it. Collies cannot be trained by repetition. They will learn a routine as quickly as they can, but if practice continues once the drill is perfect, they lose interest. Because he tries so very hard, he does not understand the "jerk and yell" mentality of older training methods and will resent it. Collies must be trained with an "up" attitude, a happy voice and a minimum of correction. Show him what you want him to do, be pleased with him and he will try his best for you. One trainer at the guide dog school was unwilling to work with the Collies because he said you have to be so careful with them . . . "You can't yell at them, you can't jerk them!" he complained. I smiled and told him to think about it; he didn't NEED to do those things to a Collie. Just relax and enjoy! Now he loves training them. Another guide dog trainer with a great deal of experience said he loved Collies, "You just put them in a position to learn, and you let them!"

Collies can be very stubborn when they know they are right. Whenever one of our Collies refuses a command, we never reprimand him but try to discover the reason for his refusal.

THE COLLIE AS SKEPTIC

Collies never "assume" something is always acceptable. You may have allowed someone in your home once, or told your Collie someone was "all right," but that doesn't mean at a later time or circumstance he will assume the person is still "all right." Even if you had been obviously friendly and glad to see the person, the Collie will still challenge her next time. The challenge may be no more than stepping into their path, which usually works for a relative or neighbor. However, if the person appeared unsavory in some way, the Collie would not hesitate to repel them with any force required.

Collies can be reserved and might need to be introduced to new people more than once before accepting them.

It may be rather embarrassing when your Collie won't let someone familiar back in the house until he is satisfied after repeated visits that they do belong. A homeowner, breaking into his own locked home, met a determined and menacing Collie and had some quick explaining to do! However, sometimes you could be really grateful for this trait. My friend had been letting a neighbor's son do some house repair, and woke up one night to find he had broken into her home. Her Collie, sleeping beside her, knew this man and had seen him repeatedly inside the home, but instantly attacked him. The man escaped, but was apprehended later that night.

On another occasion, a friend talked a local police officer into letting her put her Collie through the defensive training used with police canines. The "agitator," in padded arm shield and chest pad, tried to get the dog to attack, but the bemused Collie just watched him carefully. My friend explained he would have to act like he was going to attack her before the Collie would become defensive. He came at her as if to strike her, yelling loudly, thrusting out his padded arm for the Collie to grab. Instead, the Collie, thinking his mistress was in danger, ducked under the padded arm and went upward toward the man's throat. Only a quick command on her part stopped what could have been a bad situation. Although the Collie was not invited back, his proud mistress knew that her dog would always find a way to protect her. Never underestimate the Collie's desire or ability to guard his human flock.

The Collie still retains the instinct and talent to herd. Shown here is the blue merle, Ch. Millknock Sparks Will Fly, HT, PT, working sheep with his co-owner, Marianne Sullivan.

As herding dogs, Collies do not like uncontrolled speed around them. This includes motorcycles, skateboards, roller skates, bicycles and even lawn tractors.

Collies have actually tried to grab the tires to stop what they saw as a danger. Unless your Collie has been given excellent training in voice control and someone is with him at all times, he should be in a fenced yard or on leash.

THE STOIC COLLIE

Collies are very stoic and often hide pain. Veterinarians are used to my explanations that a dog is sick because I can see it in his face. Although we often joke about this, they take me very seriously because I have never been wrong. Often when the veterinarian is watching for pain reaction, the Collie is bravely bearing the pain. It is very important to form a rapport with your beloved pet, learning to read his facial and body language both for everyday contact and emergencies.

Owners need to be observant, as a Collie is good at hiding any symptoms of physical pain.

SOCIAL AND SMART

Intelligent Collies learn to milk situations for all they're worth. One of our Collies needed to have an infected toenail removed and the foot bandaged. When the bandage was removed, he continued limping. After being assured there was nothing wrong, I bandaged another foot, and he stopped limping on the injured paw and started limping on the bandaged one. Finally, our only way to solve the problem was to bandage all four feet— that worked.

While Collies don't roam, they are sociable and will often visit neighbors while you are away. Again, the best plan is to keep him in the house or in a fenced yard. I once got a call from a neighbor who laughed and told me my "longhaired hippy son" was down at her place, begging cookies. Rather startled, I went down to her home only to find our Collie Patrick had lifted the gate latch and gone visiting. On one Halloween, I got a call from another neighbor. The side gate had been left open and two of our Collies were going door to door, trick or treating with a group of neighborhood kids and having the time of their lives.

Collies can open latches and sometimes even turn doorknobs. Their long noses and bright minds soon get the hang of flipping up a gate latch, but they have learned to manage much more complicated locks requiring the proper pushing and pulling of various parts to get the gate to open. Don't take chances, be sure locks are Collie-proof.

The Rough Collie is justly famed for his beautiful coat. Happily, it is not difficult to look after.

What You Should Know About a Collie's Coat

The Collie's harsh outer coat sheds dirt so that regular brushing keeps him sparkling clean. That outer hair together with his soft wooly undercoat forms a weather-resistant double coat that also sheds water and insulates him from both heat and cold. The wooly undercoat that provides warmth in the winter, loosens and sheds out for summer, allowing spaces that trap air to help keep the dog cooler. Although the original sheepdog had to withstand all extremes of weather, today's companion Collie does not usually face that existence and deserves to be warm and secure inside the home with his family during bad weather.

Because of this double coat, regular grooming is required. Chapter 6 will cover the details, but be prepared for the fact that a Collie requires some minimum regular maintenance. If you object to the regular

presence of dog hair around your home and aren't
willing to groom as needed, you don't want a Collie.
Invest in a ShopVac™ type vacuum cleaner and
check out some of the grooming tools that can be
attached directly to the vacuum. Learn to use the
grooming tips in chapter 6 to make caring for your
Collie easier. The many joys of living with a Collie
make it all worthwhile.

More Information on Collies

NATIONAL BREED CLUB

The Collie Club of America, Inc.
Ms. Carmen Leonard, Secretary
1119 S. Fleming Road
Woodstock, IL 60098

OTHER ORGANIZATIONS

The Collie Club of America
Foundation, Inc.
47 Wicks End Lane
Wilton, CT 06897

American Working Collie Association
Ms. Lisa King
5906 Weki County Road 18
Longmont, CO 80504

Canine Eye Registry Foundation (CERF)
South Campus Court, Building C
West Lafayette, IN 47907

Orthopedic Foundation for Animals
2300 Nifong Boulevard
Columbia, MO 65201

RECOMMENDED BOOKS

Many of these can be found on the Internet or in
breed magazine advertisements if not available
through your local bookstores.

The Collie Club of America. *The New Collie.* New York:
Howell Book House, 1996.

Roos, Mrs. George H. "Bobbee." *Collie Concept,* revised edition. Loveland, Colo.: Alpine Publications, Inc., 1988.

———*The Collective Writings of Bobbee Roos.* The Collie Club of America Foundation, 1998.

Starkweather, Patricia Roberts, with John Buddie. *The Magnificent Collie.* Wilsonville, Ore.: Doral Publishing, Inc., 1997.

Sundstrom, Harold and Mary. *Collies, A Complete Pet Owner's Manual.* Hauppauge, N.Y.: Barron's Educational Series, Inc.

RECOMMENDED MAGAZINES

AKC GAZETTE, The Official Journal for the Sport of Purebred Dogs, 260 Madison Avenue, New York, NY 10016.

THE COLLIE CLUB OF AMERICA BULLETIN, official publication of the Collie Club of America, 47 Wicks End Lane, Wilton, CT 06897.

COLLIE EXPRESSIONS, P.O. Box 149, Manassas, VA 20108.

RECOMMENDED VIDEOS

Collies. American Kennel Club/Video Fulfillment, Suite 200, 5580 Centerview Drive, Raleigh, NC 27606.

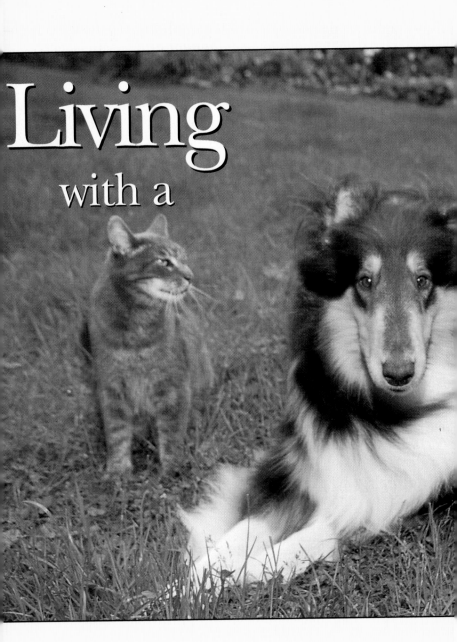

Living

with a

part two

Collie

chapter 4

Bringing Your
Collie
Home

Buying a puppy is an emotional experience. That charming puppy can grow into a most wonderful dog; she deserves your full time, love and attention to her needs. Many shelter or rescue dogs have behavioral problems because no one spent the time to socialize them properly or teach them manners. Acquiring a Collie should never be impulsive; it is devoting many years to what can be one of the most rewarding things you will ever do.

Before You Bring the Puppy Home

Before making the big decision, be sure you do your homework. Most grocery shoppers will squeeze, scrutinize, and examine an item before buying. Most puppy buyers just grab and hug. Before becoming emotionally involved, do some examining. Some simple steps can help you make that purchase one that enriches your and your family's life for years.

LEARN ABOUT THE BREED

Talk to Collie owners; are they happy? What would they change? Visit a dog show and watch how Collies interact with people and other dogs. Chat with owners or handlers after judging, get acquainted with the dogs. Beware of people who only tell you the good side. Breeders who love their breed want puppies in homes where they will be loved and wanted; they want no surprises that could cause problems later. Others just want to make a quick sale. Read books like this one that tell you everything you should know about Collies. Talk to one or more veterinarians. Visit local obedience classes and just observe. Again, ask if you can pet a dog you particularly like, and try to pick a time the dog is not being trained. Be sure the Collie is in tune with your personality and lifestyle.

FIND A RESPONSIBLE BREEDER

The best source for a quality Collie puppy is from a hobby breeder. It takes years of experience, study and work to raise good dogs. Personal referrals are the best path to the right breeder. Seek someone others have had successful dealings with.

While making your inquiries about the breed, also ask knowledgeable people to recommend breeders. Many vets, groomers, boarding kennels and pet stores have copies of listings from local breeder referral groups. The American Kennel Club will give you the name of the current Secretary for the Collie Club of America (CCA), who will direct you to the District Director in your state. The directors have a listing of all the CCA members in your area, and usually a good general knowledge of who might have puppies. This contact person should also be able to advise you on common health and genetic problems, how Collies do in your local climate and on the basic questions you as a prospective Collie owner will have.

Select a breeder who is helpful, interested in you and your reasons for wanting a Collie and who is full of details about the personalities and characteristics of the puppies, the parents and the breed—a sure indication he is in it for the love of the Collie. He should ask you questions that help determine if you will be a successful Collie owner, just as you will ask him questions about his dogs.

Visiting a dog show is a good way to locate breeders who may have puppies of the age, sex and color you want to find.

Remember, you and the puppy must operate as a team; your breeder and your vet are a crucial part of this partnership.

Review the sales contract and be sure you both understand every item. Ask questions. What is the policy if the puppy develops a health or genetic problem after the purchase? Read chapter 7 and familiarize yourself with breed-specific health issues. Be wary of breeders who imply their dogs have no problems. Rather, look for a breeder who will explain what problems occur in Collies and what he does to avoid or manage them. What is the breeder's policy if you can no longer keep your Collie? Responsible breeders' contracts always guarantee that if special needs arise and no other good home is available, or in emergencies such as a death or illness in the family, divorce or other problems, the Collie can be returned to them.

Starting Off Right

Your new puppy should have a health certificate detailing her inoculations and worming record and when her next shots are due. You should also receive eye examination results from a board-certified ophthalmologist certifying that your puppy is free of any potential vision problems. (Many Collies have some degree of a syndrome called "Collie Eye Anomaly," see chapter 7.) At the same time you will be given a pedigree, registration certificate or application and history of health clearances along with a feeding schedule and other information the breeder wants to pass on.

See your veterinarian within a few days to have the new puppy checked over and to set up regular visits to continue her shots, start her on heartworm preventive and check on her general health and progress (refer to chapter 7) for more details.

Choices, Choices, Choices

The best age to introduce the youngster into your home is between 8 and 14 weeks. This is when puppies make the transition best; they are open for learning and socialization, and they are cute as a button, but they do require a lot of attention and care. Older, properly socialized puppies are great, but it is imperative that a puppy be exposed to strangers, noise and new locations at a fairly early age if she is to cope with the world later on. Sometimes wonderful adult Collies are available through rescue groups or shelters. The reasons are as many as the stories are poignant.

Male or female? This is not really a big decision with Collies. The males are equally as sweet and caring as the females. Both sexes are devoted to children and make good guard dogs, quickly learning to discriminate among visitors. Spaying or neutering is recommended so that the Collie's full attention can be devoted to the human family.

Coat and color? Collies offer a kaleidoscope of colors and markings, and two coat varieties to suit any taste. Don't just demand a Lassie look-alike. All the colors are glorious, and the elegant Smooth variety may fit your busy lifestyle, your environment or your artistic taste perfectly. The Rough Collie's coat is her crowning glory, but it requires regular, consistent grooming to remain that way. Be deliberate and be practical.

All Collie colors are attractive, and the prospective buyer should keep an open mind on this point when seeking a puppy.

Preparing for the Collie Puppy

Consider all the things around your house and yard your puppy can get into. Check toxic or poisonous plants that might be growing there. Is the fence secure? Collies need to be fenced; as herding dogs they will chase moving vehicles they see as a danger. Puppies chew, so pick up anything potentially harmful, and be sure the puppy's outside time is supervised at first to insure she doesn't discover anything you missed. Be particularly careful that no poisons or pesticides are within her reach. Fertilizers can be dangerous, and just a few drops of antifreeze can cause a painful death. Take no chances; purchase the new formulation that is safe for animals if swallowed.

Indoors, again, puppies are chewers. Like human infants, anything and everything goes into their mouths, so follow good rules of "child-proofing"—eliminate all potential dangers before they become problems. Many popular houseplants such as poinsettia, philodendron, dieffenbachia, caladium, spider plant, azalea and oleander are toxic. Pesticides, bleach, cleaning fluids and medicines are all targets for an inquisitive puppy. Raising a puppy takes a lot of time and effort, but the Collie puppy is fun and soon enough will be well on her way to responsible adulthood.

BE CRATE-SMART

Most people today use crate-training to protect a puppy and the environment by keeping her from harm (and temptation) until she can be trained. Choose a crate that will fit the grown Collie; it is roomy enough for the puppy and her toys, food and water and she won't outgrow it. My personal preference is a

Collie puppies have a talent for mischief. Be sure to show your new puppy what is and is not allowed in your household.

portable, folding wire crate. Fiberglass airline-types retain body heat and keep the dog from seeing out, and you from seeing in. I like the kind that can also be opened from the top so you can reach the dog in an emergency and leave the top open in normal use as a pen.

Large beach towels, baby blankets and comforters for bedding are soft, washable and inexpensive if the puppy teethes on them. Once the puppy is past the chewing stage, you can use a dog bed or crate pad; many of these are washable also.

Some people are uncomfortable with "caging" the puppy. Crates are not cages, they are bedrooms. Dogs don't like to soil their sleeping areas, and the puppy will make every attempt to keep her "room" clean as soon as she is physically able. The crate should never be used as punishment, and the puppy should be taken out often for playtime and visiting. Our Collies nap in their open crates, and although they each have their own crate, they sometimes just swap. If it seems to be a mutual decision, I just go along with it, and usually they swap back again later on.

EXERCISE PENS

If someone is home all the time to watch and work with the puppy, you can probably do just fine with one crate. However, in a working household where there are long intervals when the puppy will be left alone, you might want to consider an "exercise pen." These 4-foot square portable pens are usually about 3 to 4 feet high. They can be set up indoors, on a porch or in the yard to provide a safe play area for the puppy. Purchase a remnant of linoleum larger than

the pen to protect the floor, and stabilize the pen so she cannot shove the sides around. For the outdoors, special pins can be pushed into the ground to keep the pen secure, but indoor use may need some planning. Two sides can be temporarily secured to kitchen cabinets, or small eyes tacked to the baseboard will fasten it down.

Since you will be leaving the puppy for extended periods, she will probably have to relieve herself; place several layers of newspaper in one corner for her to use until she is old enough to last until you get back. Young puppies should not be closed off in the bathroom or kitchen unless you are ready for the worst. Once your puppy is older, use baby gates to secure her in dog-friendly rooms while protecting other areas of the home.

PROBLEM PREVENTION

The whole family must participate in the puppy's education. Young children must pick up their toys or risk losing them. Shoes kicked off carelessly and clothes dropped haphazardly become easy targets for a puppy who has no idea they are not fair game. Anything plastic seems to entice chewing; ballpoint pens, CD covers, battery radios, combs and hairbrushes. Although children can be assigned various puppy chores, it must always be an adult's responsibility to be sure they get done. Watch bathroom and kitchen; trashcans and garbage cans are wonderful sources of things to get into, and deodorant soaps are toxic. We had a puppy pull a long line of toilet paper throughout the whole house, never tearing it loose, wrapping it around chairs and tables with great pride.

Some owners give their dogs open beds. But be sure there is nothing in the bed that will hurt it if the bed is chewed on.

Training Tips

Teach the puppy her limits and be consistent. Letting a puppy growl or nip because it is cute leads to an adult dog that assumes it's okay to growl and nip. Treat the puppy with respect and courtesy and always correct fairly. Have house rules for the kids that her crate is off-limits and her rest time is not to be disturbed. No teasing, no kidding.

Collies are very in tune to the spoken word, body language, facial expressions, emotions and tone of voice. They will try very hard to figure out what you want and do it. Excessive or harsh corrections will destroy the partnership. Generally, a simple "no," a distracting noise or a change of location will be all that is required to stop an annoying action. While Collies object to criticism, they do respond to praise. Heap it on! If your puppy is doing something wrong, simply say "no" and when she stops, praise immediately. If she resumes the behavior, a firmer "no" or even removing her to another location may be necessary.

Collies are "people" dogs and are at their best when they can relate fully to their human families.

Teach her the "names" of people and objects in your home. Collies soon learn to identify family members by name, various toys, activities, and so on. Collies, being quite vocal, often will "talk" right back, going through long doggie-equivalent conversations with you, especially if you've been gone. When we lived on acreage, the Collies would carry messages fastened to their collars to family members simply by being told, "Go find whomever."

SOCIALIZING YOUR DOG

Your Collie needs ample human companionship, so take her with you in the car, to the park, through an outdoor mall; find reasons and places to do things with your puppy. Don't combine these excursions with shopping trips. Puppies should never be left unattended in a car while you run into a store.

Before a car trip, be sure the puppy has only a light meal. Have her look out the closed window at the exciting sights passing by. Stop frequently and let her have a short trip outside so she associates car rides with fun. Take water and a bowl, paper towels, her leash, of course, and sandwich bags if you must clean up behind her. Make it a habit to put a few paper towels inside sealable sandwich bags; carry these in your pocket on walks, or in the car, for emergencies. Make the trips short, fun and often. She'll soon be hooked on the fun of joyriding.

Supplies

Shopping for supplies for the new puppy can be an adventure. Pet shops sell every conceivable type of toy, brush, bowl and treat. Make a list and purchase the basics first. Add to these as your puppy grows and you find out what she likes and doesn't like. Because your puppy will be growing rapidly, use common sense in your purchases so you do not keep replacing expensive items. Toys that squeak or bounce, some dog biscuits to chew on and a stuffed bunny or bear to snuggle are the basics. Dog supplies can be purchased in stores everywhere and mail-order catalogs offer everything from crates to sweaters. Do some price comparisons, as there is a wide range of costs for many items.

COLLARS AND LEASHES

Select an adjustable flat buckle collar, or an adjustable snap-on type, and check it often for fit. Many of these are washable and can be coordinated in matching colors to the leash. I prefer a lightweight, 6-foot leash. Choose a fairly narrow collar so you do not flatten the coat down around the throat. Once the Collie approaches mature size, invest in a rolled leather collar. You should be able to fit two fingers between the collar and the puppy's neck for a proper fit. Do not leave the collar on the puppy when you are not with her; accidents can and do happen. Keep the collar and leash near the front door for ready access at any time.

Always be consistent in training. Correcting a puppy for a behavior one time and ignoring it the next is sure to result in a confused, unhappy and unreliable adult house dog.

Make wearing the collar an occasion; you are going out to play, or for a drive or a walk. Collie puppies soon adjust to the collar. After she starts taking it for granted, clip on a lightweight leash and let her drag it around. Help her get it untangled when it catches and keep telling her how much fun she's having. Pick it up and follow her around, then put a little gentle pressure on the leash and call her. Have some treats ready and encourage her to follow you by voice and by slapping the side of your leg invitingly. Herding breeds seem to understand leash training fairly quickly and take to it readily. By nature, they like walking with their owners, going places and seeing people and objects of interest.

Collies are normally quite vocal, a trait which stems from their working background. Herding dogs often use voice and action to move and control livestock.

FOOD AND WATER DISHES

Collies also have a real sense of humor and an inquisitive nature; for example, they delight in flipping over their food and water bowls and the noise they can make bouncing them around. Purchase bowls that are weighted and larger at the bottom so your dog can't get her nose or foot under the lip. Use fairly deep water bowls and fill only to the bottom third. This makes a

dog raise her head before walking off and that last drop can fall in the bowl. Collie puppies often drink on the run and will not finish swallowing that last drop.

TOYS

Buy real "dog" toys, not human baby toys, because they are made of materials that will not harm the puppy if she swallows them. Homemade toys also work well. A squeaky toy wrapped in an old sock, stuffed into another sock and knotted off is a delight for a puppy to chew and carry around. Giving a puppy a sock for a toy will not make it chew socks. In fact, a puppy can be told "no" when she chews on a good sock, have it taken away and one of her own substituted. And she seems to readily grasp the difference. A clean plastic milk jug with a few beans inside and the top fastened securely will rattle and bang enough to please any Collie. Your Collie will toss and catch these by the handle, rattle them and have a ball. Watch that she does not chew on the plastic or swallow any of it.

Never tease your puppy with her toys, and insist that she release them to you if asked. Always give them right back, or if you need to take something away from her, give her something back so she won't feel possessive. Hold some toys back for special times, like when you are leaving, as a key to "quiet time."

Generally, Collies are not natural retrievers. They will chase a ball, even stop it, but they must be encouraged to pick it up and bring it back, so start early to roll a ball and get your puppy to bring it back. Make this a fun, exciting game, and later you can teach her to fetch all kinds of things. My children always love to tell about when they were growing up. They would throw a stick for Patrick who would run over and show them where it landed, and they would go get it, throw it again and encourage him to chase it. He would again run over and show them where it landed. After several sessions they realized that this WAS the game; he had taught them to throw and retrieve!

Daily Scheduling

Deciding on a daily routine and sticking to it are the keys to a happy relationship. Ideally, someone should be with the puppy constantly, at least during the first few days. Plan to bring the puppy home with at least a long weekend to settle in. If you must be gone, perhaps to work, then maybe a neighbor, friend or relative could come by and check on her, take her outside for a romp and potty time, some fresh water and some treats, so she doesn't feel abandoned.

Things usually go along pretty well until bedtime that first night. Plan ahead. Place the crate beside the bed so she will know you are nearby and reassure her she is with "family."

PUPPY HOUSETRAINING

Puppy bladders are really tiny. Again, plan ahead, don't allow the puppy to fill up on food and water just before bedtime. Take her outside for a last trip just before you put her to bed, and be prepared to get up during the night for a few days, but usually the pup is soon sleeping through the night (and rising with the dawn!).

No matter how much you enjoy sleeping later in the morning, if you want a housetrained dog you must get up and take her out as soon as she wakes. If you have a fenced yard, carry her outside, place her on the ground and as soon as she has relieved herself, praise her mightily and let her walk back inside with you. The reason for carrying her out is so she won't get a chance to make a mistake in the house and gets the idea that you think it is important to hurry outside first thing. Bring her back inside, make her breakfast and as soon as she has eaten, out she goes again because she will shortly have a bowel movement if she didn't earlier. If you don't have a fenced yard, be sure to use her collar and leash while you are out together.

Invest in a good pooper scooper—a handy little item that allows you to clean up behind the puppy without having to bend. This shovel/rake combination is a real life saver for convenience and speed.

When the puppy is making some headway on house-training, begin letting her have some house time. Collies are one of the easiest and fastest breeds to housetrain, and they get housetraining basics down pat very fast. Lots of play, lots of praise, some snacks and it's naptime. Back in the crate, toys, some snuggly bedding and a quiet place away from what's going on is best. When she wakes up, she will cry to go out, and you repeat the routine. You and the puppy will soon settle into the routine, and as she grows, she will be able to go longer between potty trips and will also learn to head for the door when she feels the need. Be very attentive while playing, as young puppies become so involved in their play they suddenly realize they need to go and whoops, it's too late. Be alert if the puppy suddenly starts sniffing around or circling. If the puppy has been involved in active play for several minutes, take her outside as she'll probably need to go. Use some word, such as "outside" or even "potty," so she associates it with relieving herself; it will be handy in new circumstances, areas or traveling to let the dog understand what you want.

SPEND SOME TIME TRAINING, SOME JUST GETTING ACQUAINTED

Spend indoor and outdoor time, sometimes just sitting in the front yard with the puppy on leash and letting her watch the world go by. Don't worry about leash training too early; rather, work to establish a relationship so she wants to be with you. Walk around together, talk to her and now and then give her a treat. Soon she will be walking with you, and the rest is easy.

Remember the socializing we talked about earlier? Walk her up and down the block a short distance; teach her not to go toward the street. Walk her around the yard and teach her the yard perimeter. Use a special word whenever you step outside the boundaries so she learns to stay in her yard unless invited outside.

Use treats to encourage the puppy to keep her attention on you. A handful of goodies dropped into your pocket and doled out along the way keeps her attention always partially on you so she is always ready for a signal or command. Use lots of conversation, too, as Collies seem to have a great capacity for understanding human speech, not just command words. Remember, she will be the very best friend and most adoring partner you could ever want—give her every opportunity to think the same of you.

chapter 5

Feeding

Your

Collie

The modern dog food industry abounds with many brands and formulas; you name it, someone has put it in a dog food! TV ads claim their product is the very best; magazine ads show successful breeder testimonials; and everyone has a favorite you cannot top. There are premium designer feeds at premium prices, low-priced generic feeds claiming to be complete, and everything in between. So how do you go about picking out the best diet?

While there is no one "right" food for your Collie, there are certainly "better" foods for your dog, depending on age, size, activity level, condition and even breed characteristics and family inheritance. The Collie is a large, fairly active breed, but adapts easily to suburban and city living. Feeding a high-energy, high-fat food to a dog whose only activity is rounding up the family cat and watching TV with the kids quickly leads to obesity. Feeding your dog what you think he would like, rather than what is best for him, leads to health problems and susceptibility to diseases. Dogs do not need or crave variety in their meals and are perfectly happy on one daily diet. However, what this diet provides is the key to a happy, healthy Collie.

Learn to Read the Labels

What makes one dog food better than another? Reading the ingredients list is a start, but feeding trials tell even more. Dogs absorb nutrients from the ingredients in the food. Thus, key words like "digestibility" become important. The quality of the food involves the amount of nutrients the dog derives from it.

Nutrients necessary for your dog's health and development include carbohydrates, fats, proteins, minerals, vitamins and water. Only a certain portion of a particular ingredient will be absorbed and used by the dog. If you feed a quality food, it will have a higher digestibility and the dog will utilize more nutrients per volume of food (bioavailability).

Generic brands may have the same list of ingredients, but their poorer quality means they may be harder to digest and therefore offer less nutritional value. Premium dog foods are termed "nutrient dense." You might pay more, but you feed

HOW TO READ THE DOG FOOD LABEL

With so many choices on the market, how can you be sure you're feeding the right food to your dog? The information's all there on the label—if you know what you're looking for.

Look for the nutritional claim right up top. Is the food "100% nutritionally complete?" If so, it's for nearly all life stages; "growth and maintenance," on the other hand, is for early development; puppy foods are marked as such, as are senior foods.

Ingredients are listed in descending order by weight. The first three or four ingredients will tell you the bulk of what the food contains. Look for the highest-quality ingredients, like meats and grains, to be among them.

The Guaranteed Analysis tells you what level of protein, fat, fiber and moisture are in the food, in that order. While these numbers are meaningful, they won't tell you much about the quality of the food. Nutritional value is in the dry matter, not the moisture content.

In many ways, seeing is believing. If your dog has bright eyes, shiny coat, a good appetite and a good energy level, chances are his diet's fine. Your dog's breeder and your veterinarian are good sources of advice if you're still confused.

less! A dog food can have all the right ingredients, but if the dog cannot digest them fully, then they do not provide what they appear to promise.

TYPES OF FOODS/TREATS

There are three types of commercially available dog food—dry, canned and semisoft—and a huge assortment of treats (lucky dogs) to feed your dog. Which should you choose?

Dry and canned foods contain similar ingredients. The primary difference between them is their moisture content. The moisture is not just water; it's blood and broth, too, the very things that dogs adore. So while canned food is more palatable, dry food is more economical, convenient and effective in controlling tartar buildup. Most owners feed a 25% canned/75% dry diet to give their dogs the benefit of both. Just be sure your dog is getting the nutrition he needs (you and your veterinarian can determine this).

Semi-moist food has the flavor dogs love and the convenience owners want. However, they tend to contain excessive amounts of artificial colors and preservatives.

Dog treats come in every size, shape and flavor imaginable, from organic cookies shaped like postmen to beefy chew sticks. Dogs seem to love them all, so enjoy the variety. Just be sure not to overindulge your dog. Factor treats into his regular meal sizes.

Selection, Selection, Selection

Most confusion arises over terminology—growth diets, maintenance diets, all-purpose diets. Identify the purpose of the food to determine its use. Puppy and growth foods are formulated to support proper growth and health in dogs from weaning to adulthood. They generally have more protein, fat, calcium and phosphorus critical to a young dog's growth. Maintenance foods provide adequate nutrition for the mature dog in an average home environment. All-purpose foods meet or exceed the nutrient requirements for all stages from puppyhood to old age.

Puppies should generally stay on a growth formula until they reach about 90 percent of their expected adult weight. However, most puppies would do nicely on a quality all-purpose food. High-energy, super-premium foods for very active dogs have high caloric density and can cause obesity in less active pets.

Collies can vary considerably, both in size and weight. Some spend a lot of easy, quiet time; others run and play and stay active. Older pets have different needs. Genetic characteristics such as a tendency to leanness, to weight gain, to laziness or hyperactivity also count. Some dogs use their food more efficiently. So the bottom line is based on how the dog looks and acts. If he is an eager eater, bright, alert and healthy, with a firm body, an inner glow and enthusiasm, the diet is obviously doing a good job.

Water

Cool, clean water should be available at all times. Collies, because of their long muzzles, will sometimes drip water around the bowl as they finish drinking. Buckets filled only to the bottom third allow water to drain back as the dog raises his head, eliminating any mess. Many dogs also enjoy licking or chewing ice cubes.

Storing Dog Food

Dry dog food keeps best in the original bag, which has a special inner liner to prevent fat from evaporating and to keep the food fresh. Additionally, the bag should be kept tightly closed and in a cool, dry place. For convenience, this bag can be placed inside a plastic storage container and kept in a convenient food preparation area. The top should close securely and the bag inside should also be tightly closed to preserve the food's freshness and content.

Feeding Your Puppy

Your new Collie puppy will have been weaned and started on a premium puppy food before you bring him home, usually with a list of instructions from the breeder. He will probably be at least 8 weeks old and able to eat dry dog food. Now is the time to make some "house rules" and stick to them. If you spoil the puppy now, he will grow into a finicky eater. Feeding time is a special bonding time; you are showing

HOW MANY MEALS A DAY?

Individual dogs vary in how much they should eat to maintain a desired body weight—not too fat, but not too thin. Puppies need several meals a day, while older dogs may only need one. Determine how much food keeps your adult dog looking and feeling his best. Then decide how many meals you want to feed with that amount. Like us, most dogs love to eat, and offering two meals a day is more enjoyable for them. If you're worried about overfeeding, make sure you measure correctly and abstain from adding tidbits to the meals.

Whether you feed one or two meals, only leave your dog's food out for the amount of time it takes him to eat it—10 minutes, for example. Freefeeding (when food's available any time) and leisurely meals encourage picky eating. Don't worry if your dog doesn't finish all his dinner in the allotted time. He'll learn he should.

the puppy he is welcome in your home and family. His food is his, his mealtime is his private time; keep distractions away and let him eat calmly. Let this also be "crate time" so he understands playtime is over, distractions are gone and he can focus on eating. Giving him some quiet, private time also encourages him to not bolt his food. Give the same word cues to tell him that it is *his* feeding time. Perhaps a cheerful, "Hungry?" is all he needs. This pays off later, perhaps during outside activities that upset the daily routine, when these words will cue him to what you expect of him.

For a young puppy, first soak the dry food in warm water for a few minutes, then stir. Once he has teeth, a puppy can manage dry food nicely, but soaking makes the food easier for him to chew and releases enticing odors. Healthy puppies generally clean their bowls eagerly. Feed the amount he will readily finish, and remove the dish after about fifteen to twenty minutes whether the food is gone or not. Collies easily become "snackers," returning to the food bowl for a few bites as they please. Puppyhood is the best time to discourage that undesirable, unhealthy habit.

I usually start puppies on three meals a day and a small snack before bedtime. This last can be just some dog biscuits, baby carrots or another healthy nibble in his crate as you put him to bed for the night. A large meal late in the evening defeats housetraining. Generally time the three feedings around your family's regular mealtimes. In today's busy world, no one may be home for that middle feeding. While this is not ideal, you can work around it. After the morning meal and exercise, put the puppy in his crate or pen along with his dry dog food and some dog biscuits, and he will eat it when he gets hungry. Always be sure there is plenty of water available, some toys, a radio tuned to a talk show for company, and some comfy bedding.

Follow the feeding advice of your puppy's breeder at first. If you want to change the food or the feeding schedule, be sure to do so gradually.

Puppies generally show less interest in the middle meal as their frantic growth spurt slows, probably at around 6 to 7 months of age, and can be cut back to morning and evening meals. Feed early enough so the puppy's system has time to process the last meal and relieve himself before bedtime.

TEACH YOUR PUPPY TO SHARE

Very young children think nothing of invading the dog's dinner bowl. While most Collies happily share, new owners should think ahead and teach the puppy to allow them to remove food from his mouth with no resistance. Once the puppy has settled in and is comfortable with everyone and the family's routine, start training him to allow you to handle his food bowl. Sit on the floor beside the food bowl while he is eating and gently lift the bowl, setting it in your lap. Allow him to finish eating while you assure him everything is quite normal. Never do this teasingly, but very matter of factly. Handle him around his face, scratch behind his ears, touch his feet, but make sure you do not interfere with his eating. Later, give him a treat large enough for you to hold while he chews on his end. Again, pet him, reassure him, maybe even take the treat back and return it to him.

He should watch you with anticipation but no aggression. If he resists, holding onto his treat, then quietly and firmly open his mouth enough to remove the treat, use a command such as "Release," and take the goodie. Tell him how wonderful he is, hold the treat where he can continue to see it and then return it to him with much praise. If you do this fairly often, he will patiently allow you to take anything he has, knowing you will return it. This little trick may save his life someday if he picks up something dangerous you must take away from him.

Feeding the Adult Collie

Most Collies reach adult size at around 9 months of age. He will continue to mature for several months, but the frantic growth spurt should be over. Now is the time to gradually switch him to a quality adult maintenance food.

Feeding schedules depend on the routine of the household and the needs of the dog. Young adults probably do better on two smaller meals a day, while older, mature dogs often thrive on one meal. If the family sits down to regular meals, the dog will also anticipate being fed. If the family is gone during the day, try a small snack in the morning and a full early evening meal, again giving him ample time to relieve himself before bedtime.

Your Collie's overall condition is the key to how well he is being fed.

Deciding how much to feed can be tricky to start. Use manufacturer's guidelines, but remember, they are only guidelines. Premium feeds require smaller quantities for the same level of nutrition; dogs eat calories, not quantities. I prefer the smaller size kibble that does not swell when soaked in water. I do not soak the adult food, but I do pour a small amount of warm water over the food just before serving to release the baked-in odors. Crunchy food helps clean teeth and remove tartar.

Young adult Collies often appear lean well into maturity. There is a difference between leanness and thinness; Collies should not be thin or unthrifty. A Collie, given the chance, will exercise, whether on long walks with his owner or at play with the family. If your Collie gains too much weight, encourage him to exercise more while cutting back slightly on his food. Feeding twice a day but with the total volume slightly reduced may help. Be sure you are feeding a maintenance diet, not an all-purpose diet. Ideally, the nutrient requirements for a dog's life stage should match the nutrient balance in the food he eats.

Table Scraps

Feeding table scraps and snacks is the leading cause of obesity because dogs soon learn to hold out for these tasty treats, often refusing their regular diets. How much is too much? Good quality commercial dog food has a built-in safety margin of essential nutrients; a small amount of meat or table scraps will not harm this balance.

Supplements

Caring owners insist on adding additional vitamins, minerals and flavorings. However, continued or excessive supplementation will destroy this margin. Avoid raw eggs, as the whites can cause a vitamin B deficiency. Cod liver oil and wheat germ oil can upset the balance of vitamin D and cause skeletal disorders. Excessive oils can interfere with the absorption of other nutrients. Adding calcium, phosphorus and other minerals to an already balanced diet can decrease the absorption of other critical minerals. Many people add additional calcium to the diet of large dogs, but this can lead to calcium oversupplementation. Excessive vitamins can cause toxic symptoms, poor growth and other problems. Meat is an excellent supplement but should be limited to not over 15 percent of the regular diet, and table scraps should be limited to not over 10 percent. Many dogs cannot digest whole milk and will develop diarrhea. Powdered milk mixed with warm water, low-fat milk or acidophilus added milk to allow digestion appear to be beneficial in limited amounts.

A recommended supplement is apple cider vinegar: a time-tested favorite. A tablespoon or two in the dog's food daily seems to promote healthy skin and coat, reduces intestinal and urinary tract infections and, as a side effect, even seems to repel fleas, though this may be a result of the healthier skin. It also seems to act as an appetite stimulant, and the dogs actually appear to enjoy it.

Polyunsaturated fats added to the dog's diet in small amounts when the coat is shedding, or during the winter months when indoor heating dries out the coat and skin, help maintain a shiny, healthy coat. Corn oil or safflower oil are high in linoleic acid essential to the canine diet and are readily available. Add these gradually and build up to no more than a tablespoon per day, as needed.

TO SUPPLEMENT OR NOT TO SUPPLEMENT?

If you're feeding your dog a diet that's correct for his developmental stage and he's alert, healthy looking and neither over- nor underweight, you don't need to add supplements. These include table scraps as well as vitamins and minerals. In fact, a growing puppy is in danger of developing musculoskeletal disorders by oversupplementation. If you have any concerns about the nutritional quality of the food you're feeding, discuss them with your veterinarian.

Snacks and Treats

Snacks may be used to optimally promote the relationship between you and your Collie. Do not use food as a reward; rather, use it as a means of directing the dog's attention to you. If the dog's attention is on you, he will generally do anything you ask.

Weight Control

Obesity was once fairly rare in Collies, but with fewer opportunities to exercise, better food and health care and indulgent owners, it is becoming a problem. Avoiding overweight is much easier than trying to slim down an overweight dog. Obesity increases risk of heart and respiratory problems, liver disease and cancer. It also increases surgical risk, shortens your pet's life and aggravates problems such as hip dysplasia and arthritis. Although "low-calorie" foods are available, it is better to first try cutting back slightly on the amount of each meal while increasing exercise and limiting snacks.

Underweight may have several causes. Some dogs just run weight off, especially young dogs left outdoors for long periods of time with nothing else to do. If your Collie is underweight, first, with your veterinarian, rule out any medical reasons, and check with the breeder for family traits. Poor eaters are usually made, not born, and hard to retrain. Break the daily ration into several small meals, adding small amounts of something tasty to stimulate eating. Chicken soup has always had great appeal to dogs, and pasta, cooked rice or oats with honey are good enhancers. Do not let the dog get too much attention by not eating or you may make the problem worse. Never think you can just wait him out; if he gets too weak or thin, then you will have a really serious problem.

Use common sense when giving snacks and treats to your Collie. Choose healthful foods, don't overdo and make him deserve the rewards you provide.

The Geriatric Collie

Large breeds mature more slowly, and their life spans are generally shorter than those of smaller breeds. Over time, a dog's metabolic rate changes. Caloric requirements decrease as much as 20 percent with aging, so diets must change to lower fat intake, particularly saturated (animal) fat. Since kidney disease is a common cause of death in older dogs, you might want to choose a food with a lower protein level to reduce the workload of ailing kidneys. Several companies make diets for the older dog. Look for the following:

65

lower protein content (from high quality sources), low fat levels, higher in fiber, with reduced sodium and phosphorus. It is essential, as your Collie ages, that you work with your veterinarian to provide your pet with a healthy, happy old age. Dental checkups are essential. Signs of aging usually start around 8 to 10 years of age, 12 years would probably be considered a Collie senior citizen, and I know of a few right now that are approaching 17 years of age. Preventive health care is one key to keeping your beloved friend as long as possible.

If your Collie is getting the right amount of food and exercise, it will show in his appearance and activity.

Foods to Avoid

Spicy foods, candies and rich pastries, and chicken, pork chop and steak bones that can splinter are all to be avoided. Fatty foods and dairy products often result in digestive upsets or diarrhea. You can solve part of the problem of those gorgeous Collie eyes staring soulfully at each mouthful you swallow by sharing the part the dog can eat. However, make NO CHOCOLATE an ironclad rule! Whether given intentionally as a treat or stolen by a canine thief, chocolate in all forms is to be avoided. While your Collie may escape serious consequences from eating chocolate in small quantities, there is always a risk, and excessive indulgence can be serious or even fatal.

chapter 6

Grooming
Your
Collie

One of dogdom's most glamorous creations, Rough or Smooth, gleaming coat of several gorgeous colors, head held proudly, eyes sparkling, Collies are magnets for admiration.

Usually a Collie's grooming needs are minimal, but they must be done regularly. It's easy to learn to do a really beautiful job, honing your skill as finely as you wish.

Both varieties have a seasonal "blow" when the undercoat loosens, requiring a lot of elbow grease for a short while. If the

undercoat is not removed, the dog looks unkempt and retains moisture, which causes itching and "hot spots." Left ungroomed, longer coats become matted, making the Collie look bad, causing sores and inviting fleas.

The "upside" of grooming is that it is a bonding time between you and your pet. You will find it very relaxing to spend this special time together. Regular grooming also alerts you to any developing skin or coat problems long before they become serious.

Grooming Essentials

Keep grooming accessories handy in a special container. Since you may use some coat dressings or flea products in spray bottles, select a container in which bottles can stand upright. Be creative and choose whatever works for you.

GROOMING TABLE OR SURFACE

Any washable covering large enough for the Collie to lie on, will protect your rug or floor from any sprays you use, hair or dirt brushed out, and let her know that a relaxing grooming session is at hand. If you prefer, purchase a grooming table for your Collie, but still teach her to lie comfortably on her side during the grooming ritual. You may be amazed at how much your Collie loves to be groomed.

BRUSHES AND COMBS

Purchase brushes and combs from a pet shop or pet supply catalog. Ask your dog's breeder for a favorite source or consult the ads in the dog magazines in your vet's office. Then write for the catalogs that interest you. Always purchase quality tools as they will last far longer and work much better than "bargain" versions.

You will need two metal combs, both with handles. Using a comb with a handle lets you flex your wrist and keep a lighter touch. One comb should have wide-set teeth, the other should have closer-set teeth for various grooming uses. Many people like combination combs—wider teeth on one end, closer-set teeth on the other. You might also want a grooming rake, like a comb but with long teeth set at an angle. These reach deep into a long coat to the undercoat, quickly removing shedding hair.

You will need three brushes, and again, purchase quality. These are a "pin" brush, a natural bristle brush and a "slicker brush." Pin brushes have metal "pins" set into a rubber base. Choose a large brush, the very weight of which gets it through the longer hair. The bristle brush looks like a hairbrush for humans and removes dirt, distributes natural oils and keeps the coat looking right. The slicker brush should be medium to large size. You can also purchase a small one, just for use behind the ears.

Grooming sessions are essential to the dog's health and appearance and they are the ideal bonding time between dog and owner.

Spray Bottles

Have several spray bottles. Write the contents on the bottles for later reference. You can use these for a conditioning mist during grooming, or a quick water mist on a hot day, or to apply other products as needed.

Scissors

Get two pairs of scissors—regular straight-edge scissors and single-edge thinning shears. A beauty supply store is an excellent place to purchase good scissors at reasonable prices. Try various models to see what feels good for you. Also, ask the clerk what beauticians usually purchase. At home, keep scissors in a sealable plastic bag to keep them safe and clean.

Add nail scissors (with two cutting blades) or a grinder to your tool kit. I like the battery-operated "mini" grinder used for woodworking. These can be purchased at a local hardware store, run on a battery pack and have variable speeds. Although a little tricky to learn to use, they virtually eliminate nail cutting accidents.

DENTAL SUPPLIES

Clean teeth keep a Collie healthy and pleasant to be near. Dogs that are started as puppies do not mind having their teeth and mouth worked on. Dental supplies for dogs can be purchased as kits at any pet store, dog supply catalog or often through your veterinarian.

INCIDENTALS

To complete your toolbox, obtain the following items: cotton swabs, cotton squares (for cleaning ears), mineral or baby oil (again, great for cleaning ears), rubbing alcohol, peroxide, medicated powder, baby powder, pyrethrin flea spray (even safe for puppies), waterless shampoo, bath lead with suction attachment (to secure dog in tub so she can't jump out), cornstarch.

Grooming Routine

There is more to Collie grooming than brushing. Make these extras a part of your weekly grooming session:

EARS

Check inside the ears. Clean the outer ear carefully with a cotton pad and warm water. Gently remove any dirt with a cotton pad dipped in alcohol. Wax or dirt deeper in the ear can be removed with a cotton swab dipped in mineral or baby oil. DO NOT penetrate the ear canal or go further into the dog's ear than you can easily see. An oily black substance in the ear, or a strong odor, generally means ear mites or an infection and should be checked by your veterinarian.

Check your Collie's ears regularly and clean them as required. Do not probe in the ear canal where you cannot see. Report any unusual discharge to your veterinarian.

EYES

Eyes should be clear and bright with no discharge. If matter has collected in the corners of the eye, gently clean it out with a soft cloth dipped in warm water. Many dogs, like people, have seasonal allergies with eye discharge, or a discharge could indicate an infection. These need to be checked by your veterinarian.

TEETH

Teach your Collie puppy very early to let you open her mouth and check her teeth. Be sure baby teeth are coming out and adult teeth growing in properly. If a baby tooth doesn't fall out, the adult tooth often comes in poorly aligned. Your veterinarian can pull any baby teeth that need removal.

Dogs must learn to tolerate having their teeth cleaned and checked at home weekly, as well as periodic dental cleanings by your veterinarian as needed to remove tartar. You may want to do this as part of the grooming process, or with the bath, but be sure to make it a regular habit. Use toothpaste made for dogs, as toothpaste

71

for humans will upset the dog's stomach. Use a regular toothbrush or a battery-powered one made for humans or buy one especially made for dogs. You can also use little "finger toothbrushes" that are worn like a thimble on your finger and make it very easy to see and feel what you are doing. In between, let the dog chew on toys and snacks that help remove plaque.

Start cleaning your Collie's teeth when she is a puppy and you can avoid a variety of health problems throughout her life.

NAILS

Collies that exercise on cement or other hard surfaces often wear their nails down naturally and require little care. However, most pets need their nails trimmed regularly. For too many pets and their owners, this is a traumatic time; the dogs struggle and fight and owners soon become daunted or even afraid to do it. Overgrown nails can cause foot problems; they can splinter or split back into the toe, they can scratch and are both uncomfortable and unsightly.

Start trimming a puppy's nails at an early age and make it a time for praise, treats and patience. Just take off a tiny bit of the tip; only do a nail or two if the puppy is resisting and return to it later. Keep it simple and successful and stop when you are ahead. No hurry; you are training for the future. If you use a grinder, gently tap each nail tip so the puppy gets used to the vibration, each session working a bit more on each nail.

Adult Collies need their nails trimmed every two to four weeks if they are not wearing down naturally. Pay particular attention to the dewclaw nails on the "wrists" as these are often forgotten. Some breeders remove dewclaws on newborns to prevent any chance of future injuries.

How to Trim Nails

Collies' nails can be dark or clear. Clear nails show their structure. Notice the pink "quick" visible through the nail. Cutting or grinding into it will be painful and the nail may bleed. Turn this nail over and notice that the tip of the nail is partially hollow; this hollow tip can be safely removed, and by comparing its alignment with the quick on this nail, you can gauge the trimming area on dark nails.

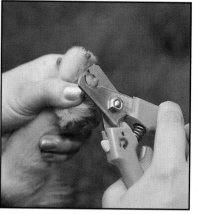

Remember, less is best until you know more. You can always trim a bit more later. Hold the foot in one hand, using your thumb and forefinger to firmly hold and extend the toe with the nail you want to trim. Cut from top to bottom, being careful to avoid the quick. Make several smaller cuts around the tip to round off the cut end, or you can use a file for ragged surfaces. Look at the cut end; if you can see a pinpoint of pink, do not cut any farther as that is the beginning of the quick.

Trim your Collie's nails at regular intervals; they will remain short and your dog will be more comfortable as a result of your good care.

Use a grinder to polish off the cut nail or to grind down the nails themselves. Grinding is quicker, neater and safer. To prevent leg feathering from catching in the rotary action of the grinder, cut the toe off an infant's stocking and slip it over the dog's leg with just the foot emerging.

Grinders can get hot, so only work on a nail for short periods and pause in between. Using the slow speed, roll the grinder from one side of the nail across the top and down the other side. Do not grind in one spot and do not use excessive pressure as this can cause pain.

Continue until a slant forms on both sides of the nail pointing to the tip. Working down from the top, gently work the tip backward, checking frequently for the pink dot; stop when you see it. Polish the nails gently to remove any sharp edges and they will be safe for skin and home furnishings.

If you accidentally sever a quick, have a coagulant handy to stop bleeding. "Kwik-Stop™," a silver nitrate stick, styptic pencil or, in a pinch, even some cornstarch or flour can be used. Firm pressure applied and held to the top of the toe where the nail grows until the bleeding stops also works.

TRIMMING EXCESS HAIR

Many Rough Collies have wispy hair around their ears and face and excess hair between their toes and under their foot pads. For hair around the ears and face, brush the long hair up and use thinning scissors to trim off the ends of the hair that seems out of place. Thinning scissors won't leave cut marks but help the hair blend into the coat around it. Don't overdo, you can always cut more later.

For feet, have the Collie standing, and with the straight scissors, cut around the shape of the foot including the toenails so the foot has a neat, rounded appearance. Cut off the straggly hair at the back of the foot and leg up to the "stopper pad" on the back of the front leg, don't cut it back to the leg, just neaten it up. Brush excess hair on the back of the hocks out with the slicker brush and, using thinning shears, trim off only enough to give the leg a clean, rounded appearance.

Remove excessive hair from the inside pads of the Rough Collie's feet, cutting carefully so you don't catch the skin. Her feet will stay cleaner and less likely to pick up natural debris. Don't cut between the toes as this makes the feet look splayed.

BRUSHING

An adult Collie in full coat should be groomed at least once a week, but go through the motions with your puppy at an early age, even though there is little to groom. Make the sessions fun, short and rewarding with lots of treats and your Collie will come to look forward to them.

Rough Collies are "line brushed." Lightly mist the coat with water from your spray bottle and with your fingers and palms, gently massage this moisture into the coat. This prevents hair breakage. If the hair is dry, add a very small amount of coat conditioner to the water (too much makes the hair greasy). Starting behind the ears, brush a line of hair toward the head, use the pin brush to separate the coat along this line or part. Hold the unbrushed coat down with the other hand, take the brush and free about a quarter inch of hair along this line and again lift and brush this toward the head. Start at the roots and brush all the way to the tip. This cleans the hair shaft and distributes natural oils along the length of the hair, making it shiny and clean, and removes any dead hair or mats. Continue working in sections, brushing the hair up or forward according to how it lies naturally. Keep brushing until you've finished one whole side, spraying occasionally if the hair dries.

Line brushing, as described in the text, is the best and most thorough way to groom a Rough Collie.

Do the neck and chest the same way. The tail should be line brushed from the base, working toward the tip. When you finish, hold the tail by the tip and give it a slight shake; the hair will fall into place. For the feathering on the front legs and the skirts on the rear legs, the technique is a bit different. Starting just above the back of the foot on the front leg, and just above the hock on the rear leg, hold the hair up against the dog. Again using your pin brush, line brush by pulling the hairs down and out a few at a time. This will remove tangles and dirt, and make the feathering look twice as full.

Turn the Collie over and repeat on the other side. Let her stand and shake, then with the pin brush or bristle brush layer the coat into its natural position, working forward from the rear so that the coat retains its lift. Sprinkle some baby powder behind her ears. The hair in this area tangles easily and the powder helps prevent this. Brush out the powder, fluffing the hair to stand out around her face and ears.

Training a dog to lie on her side for grooming makes the session easier.

Handling Mats and Tangles

Watch for mats and carefully and gently remove them. Mats and tangles generally mean split ends that will be snarled tightly into a seemingly impenetrable mass. Several methods effectively remove mats. For a small mat, dust it with baby powder and work it out by hand or gently using the comb, starting on the outside farthest from the body and slowly separating the hair, moving toward the skin. If it is more extensive, soak it with a leave-in hair conditioner that binds split ends. In a few minutes, using the comb or slicker brush, begin to separate out a few hairs, again working from the outside inward. Be careful and gentle.

For a really bad mat, especially behind the ears where cutting it out would show, it is easier to work on it during the bath. About half an hour before you are going to bathe your Collie, saturate the matted areas with a cholesterol hair product. After the Collie is in the tub, start working out the mat. The cholesterol seems to make the hair slippery and the mat can often be worked out by hand, using a comb or slicker brush to pick out the hairs, working toward the skin. Once the mat is out, the cholesterol can be shampooed out during the bath.

Items for the Bath

Bath essentials for your Collie include several large, thick towels, a quality dog shampoo, sterile ophthalmic ointment, cotton balls, a jar of cholesterol, a washcloth and maybe a waterproof apron for you. You may also want a hair dryer with cool and medium settings, and I feel a spray attachment is a necessity to rinse a Collie's thick coat.

Bathing your puppy in the sink with a sprayer teaches your Collie to accept this and all grooming operations.

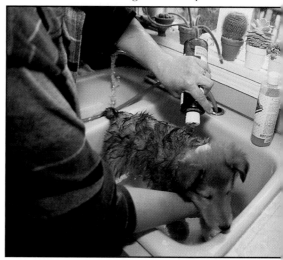

Bathing

Don't wait until your puppy is dirty to introduce her to the bath. Start early and keep it simple. Like brushing, make this fun. Have some treats available, play with her in the tub, make it quick and simple while she is small and easy to handle and your adult won't have to be dragged into the tub.

Lift each foot, handle the toes, check the ears, examine inside her mouth and use your finger to massage her teeth. You don't even need to shampoo her at these early sessions unless she needs it.

Wrap her in a big towel and make drying off a part of the play. You can introduce her to the hair dryer, on cool, just a quick once-over like a game, and touch her toenails with the clippers as you handle her feet.

77

When she is comfortable with the routine, you can give her a real bath. Always be sure she has been thoroughly brushed and checked for mats, as bathing a matted dog will only make the mats worse. Use the ophthalmic ointment in her eyes to prevent irritation, and put cotton balls in her ears so no water gets inside. Clean the inside of the ears, if needed, at this stage. Gently spray her body with warm water. The coat is water-resistant, so you won't see much progress until you add the shampoo. Using a soft cloth, gently shampoo the Collie's face. Hold her muzzle up as you rinse so water doesn't run into her nose; you may want to do this rinsing with the washcloth until she is used to it.

After the bath, many owners use a hair dryer to dry the dog and fluff out the coat.

Move from head to tail, working up a lather. Beginning at the head causes any fleas that might be on the dog to run toward the rear where they are more easily disposed of. Working toward the head allows them to hide in the Collie's ears or on her face. At this point, rinse thoroughly; this is very important. Any residual shampoo may cause itching or a rash. Be particularly careful of the underside.

Remove excess water by hand and check for remaining suds, then vigorously towel her dry. Make this fun as most dogs generally love this part. Lift a puppy out of the tub wrapped in the towel. An adult Collie can generally step out of the tub with ease, but she is going to shake.

A folding grooming table is the best place to dry your Collie. A sturdy bench works almost as well. Place her on the table to use the hair dryer and brush her dry, lifting the hair with the pin brush as you use the dryer to fluff the hair. Be sure the dryer is not too warm and keep it moving constantly. Most dogs learn to enjoy the dryer, some even lie down and take a relaxing nap at this time.

How Often to Bathe?

Bathe your Collie when she is dirty, has "doggy" odor or going into her annual shed. But are there other indications that a bath is needed? Full-time house pets are artificially exposed to longer periods of "daylight" due to inside lighting. Their internal sensors tell them it is summer, no matter what the temperature, and they may enter a phase of continual slight shedding.

Because of the Collie's size and the quantity of coat in the Rough variety, most people put off bathing until they must. Dogs "shed" because new hair is pushing old hair out as it grows in. When you delay bathing a Collie, the next bath often appears to cause copious shedding but is really the old hair that has not yet been released.

If your Collie is a house pet and you experience this continual slight shedding, bathe more often. If you use a good quality, mild dog shampoo and rinse thoroughly, you can bathe your Collie every week or two. Shampooing your pet properly does no more harm than shampooing your own hair, but it does cause the shedding hair to come out in the bath and not on your clothes or carpet. It also reduces the amount of brushing required to keep her looking right. Of course, use good common sense. In winter, allow a couple of days for the natural oils to return to her coat before allowing her outside for extended periods of time.

The Smooth Collie is easily groomed with a pin brush.

chapter 7

Keeping Your Collie Healthy

If you have selected a well-started puppy from a healthy family, you will probably experience few problems. You will need to learn the basics of good nutrition (chapter 5) and good grooming (chapter 6) to catch problems before they get a foothold. To learn about good preventive care, read on.

Finding a Veterinarian

Selecting the right veterinarian is a big first step. The breeder, if local, can make recommendations. Ask those you know with well-cared-for pets about their veterinarian. Find a doctor who will talk to you, explain things

80

and appears genuinely interested in your Collie. Ask the veterinarian about other Collie clients. The facilities need not be new, but they should be clean, well maintained and the staff courteous and caring. If you are not comfortable with a particular vet, select a new one. You must have complete trust and confidence in your choice.

What Your Puppy Needs

The breeder should have had the puppy examined by a veterinarian, and given you a record of all shots and wormings when you brought him home. Many states also require a recent health certificate. Based on the inoculations your puppy has already had, your veterinarian will set up a schedule of "puppy shots" to develop immunity against the most common diseases.

PUPPY SHOTS

Most veterinarians recommend a five-way combined shot commonly called "DHLPP" for distemper, hepatitis, leptospirosis, parvovirus, and parainfluenza. In our experience, the leptospirosis vaccine is most likely to produce bad reactions in puppies, and we generally don't give it until after the first set of shots. Several other vaccines can be included in the

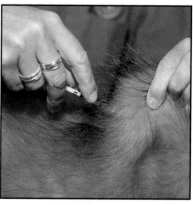

package, but we now know that the immune system of baby puppies can be easily overwhelmed at this time. Stay with the minimum necessary for your puppy's safety. Based on respected studies, we generally space vaccines on an every-three-week schedule, combined with any necessary wormings, usually starting at 7 weeks (before sale) and repeated at 10, 13 and 16 weeks of age, and then a yearly booster to maintain immunity. Rabies vaccine can be given as soon as the puppy has all his vaccinations, as many specialists do not recommend giving it with any other vaccine.

Modern veterinary science has developed many vaccines to protect your dog from most contagious diseases. Always be sure your dog's inoculations are fully current.

Internal Parasites

Internal parasites, generally worms, live mostly unseen in your unsuspecting dog. Veterinary medicine has made great strides in treatment, but internal parasites remain one of our most prevalent problems.

ROUNDWORMS

Roundworms are the most common worms seen in dogs, often infecting puppies before birth, giving them an unthrifty, pot-bellied appearance, mucoid diarrhea and slowed growth. In more severe cases they migrate to the lungs, causing pneumonia. The worms, which are often vomited or expelled in the stool, are several inches long and resemble spaghetti. Canine roundworms are transmissible to man and are a public health concern, especially in children. Puppies should be wormed before they begin shedding eggs, as early as 2 weeks old, as well as the nursing dam, who can reinfect from the puppies in a continuing circle. All stools from dam and puppies should be picked up immediately and handled with caution. Ask the breeder in advance if the puppies have been treated for roundworms, and never allow children to play with puppies that have not been wormed for roundworms or that are in unclean surroundings.

It is not uncommon for puppies to be infected with roundworms, which are passed from their mother before birth.

HOOKWORM

Hookworms, like roundworms, may be present from birth. They feed by attaching to the intestinal wall and sucking blood directly from its small vessels. Hookworm can exist all year in the soil in contaminated areas in warmer climates; in northern states they are killed by freezing weather. They can burrow directly through dogs' skin and paw pads, where they go through a similar migration as roundworms. Microscopic detection can be made twenty days after infection. Hookworms can cause acute, often fatal anemia in young puppies. Symptoms include weakness, pale gums, weight loss, dehydration, a dark, tarry stool or diarrhea containing blood and mucous.

Responsible breeders insure that bitches are worm-free before breeding, and their puppies are maintained in a sanitary environment. If your puppy needs treatment for hookworm, your veterinarian has several options.

TAPEWORM

Tapeworms are seen as flat, white or pinkish segments, are passed in the stool and are sometimes near the dog's anus. When first passed, they move, but soon dry out and resemble rice grains. Tapeworms cause an unthrifty look, dry skin, dull coat, weight loss, unusual hunger and sometimes diarrhea. Because tapeworms can migrate into dogs' anal sacs, the dog may scoot along the floor in a sitting position, trying to rub his rectum, or chase his tail in an attempt to relieve the itching.

Common internal parasites (l-r): roundworm, whipworm, tapeworm and hookworm.

Dogs generally become infected with tapeworm by ingesting fleas, the intermediary host in their life cycle. Although the veterinarian can give you several medications to remove tapeworm, the dog will continually reinfect unless you rid the premises of fleas.

WHIPWORM

Whipworm can cause anemia in the dog that will have a generally unthrifty look. Diarrhea with a particularly foul odor, often containing blood and mucous, will come and go, depending on the activity of the worms, and sometimes a routine worm check will not give evidence of eggs. Since the cycle may last up to three months, two wormings three months apart are usually required.

HEARTWORM

Because travel with dogs is routine, heartworm now exists throughout the United States and in most places where mosquitoes exist. Luckily, effective heartworm preventatives are now readily available. Puppies are usually started on heartworm preventative at around 3 to 4 months of age, and as early as 8 weeks of age in areas where heartworm is prevalent. Once-a-month products are now available, including ivermectin (Heartgard™), milbemycin oxime (Interceptor™) and moxidectin (ProHeart™).

With the addition of pyrantel to ivermectin (Heartgard Plus™), dogs can now be protected from hookworm

and roundworm. Interceptor™ alone is also effective against hookworm, roundworm and whipworm; and lufenuron was recently added to form a new product (Sentinel™) that also prevents the development of flea eggs and larvae on the dog. Consult your veterinarian for the best product for your dog.

Treating heartworm infected dogs used to be expensive, time consuming, and many dogs did not survive severe infestations. The Food and Drug Administra-

A young puppy's surroundings must be as clean as possible to protect against infective agents in the environment.

tion has recently approved melarsomine dihydrochloride (Immiticide™) which has changed the way most heartworm infected dogs are treated. It is injected into a muscle rather than into a blood vessel. An alternate-dose regimen can reduce life-threatening posttreatment complications and it is more effective at eliminating adult worms.

The once-a-month products have been found to be safe for most Collies in the low dosages used for heartworm prevention. They should never be used for treatment of a Collie for other illnesses at higher dosages. If you notice any of the following symptoms, discontinue use immediately: depression, lethargy, vomiting, bloody diarrhea, incoordination or anorexia. Change to a diethylcarbamazine citrate product given daily.

External Parasites

FLEAS

Fleas are the most common external parasite and are soon established in the environment. At the sight of even one flea, you must begin the "war." Fleas cause itching, scratching and transmit tapeworm. They also readily transfer from pet to pet owner. Dogs may develop an allergic reaction to fleabites and chew constantly at themselves from even one bite. To check for fleas on the dog, look on his stomach, his back near his tail, his face and ears and in the armpits. Flea "dirt," resembling ground pepper, may be noticed.

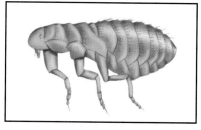

The flea is a die-hard pest.

Clean and vacuum all inside areas where the dog visits. Cut off a small piece of flea collar and put it in the vacuum bag so fleas do not set up housekeeping inside the vacuum. New products called "growth inhibitors" that prevent fleas from developing into the adult stage so they cannot reproduce are now available. Topical medications applied monthly are particularly effective for dogs. A once-a-month pill that introduces a chemical into the flea at the time of the bite prevents any eggs she lays from developing into adults. You must treat the dog, the home, the yard and the car (if he rides with you) at the same time to avoid reinfecting and continuing the cycle. Your veterinarian is your best source for the newest, best and most efficient flea prevention.

TICKS

Ticks are nasty, blood-sucking disease carriers. They are usually located on the dog's head, in and around the ears, neck, chest, top of shoulders along the spine and between toes. A single tick may be removed by grasping the tick as close to the dog's body as possible with tweezers, and using a steady, firm pressure or twisting motion to pull the tick loose.

Use tweezers to remove ticks from your dog.

LYME DISEASE AND EHRLICHIAE

Lyme disease and ehrlichiosis are tick-borne diseases. Much information has been available on Lyme disease recently, through TV, magazines and newspaper articles, but ehrlichiosis is considered a fairly new disease. Both diseases can be carried by the same tick. Canine ehrlichiosis caused the deaths of hundreds of military working dogs during the Vietnam War. These diseases are often called the "hidden killers" because so many of the symptoms go unsuspected: fever, loss of appetite, sudden pain and lameness, swollen joints, lethargy, depression, generalized infection and invasion of the joints and nervous system. If left untreated, the disease progresses to arthritis, damage to the brain, spinal chord and heart, and even the kidneys.

EAR MITES

Ear mites live in the ear canal, sucking blood and feeding off skin debris. They will produce a reddish-brown waxy excrement inside the ear, and the dog will usually scratch at the ear and often hang his head to one side. Ear mites are controlled by drops that kill the mites and help remove the waxy substance. You can also clean out the ear with a cotton swab, being careful not to go any further into the ear canal than you can see.

Inherited Diseases

Hundreds of inherited canine diseases have been documented. With new data, scientists are now identifying the locations of specific genes relating to potential problem areas. These studies are well underway in humans, and much of this knowledge has been useful to researchers in canine genetics.

Because breeds are developed from a common gene pool for specific traits, some breeds become more liable to develop "breed-specific" problems. Responsible breeders study and learn to use genetics, maintaining current knowledge of their breed's problems and how to eliminate them. Many genetic problems are "recessive," or carried unseen in the line until they match the same gene from a breeding partner, and affected puppies result. Unfortunately, not all these problems are visible or detectable early. The following are problems known to occur with some frequency within Collies. Discuss these with your breeders; they should be open and familiar with their line's background and potential and should have done any testing to insure that your puppy would be free from these problems.

EYE DISEASES

In Collies, the two most prevalent inherited eye disorders are Collie eye anomaly and progressive retinal atrophy. Puppies should be examined by a Board certified canine ophthalmologist where possible, and you should get a certificate identifying any existing problems. Dogs with totally healthy appearing eyes will be identified as "normal." You may be given a CERF certificate allowing you to register your normal-eyed Collie with the Canine Eye Registry Foundation (CERF).

Collie eye anomaly (CEA) affects approximately 85 percent of all American Collies and a lesser percentage of the breed in other countries. The mildest form does not appear to affect vision to any visible degree and does not impair an affected Collie's ability to function as a pet. Puppies' eyes can be examined by a canine ophthalmologist at 5 weeks of age to accurately determine their status. Puppies identified as normal are deemed free of the anomaly but may be genetic carriers. More severely affected puppies may have varying degrees of impaired vision and should not be purchased as pets. Avoid a puppy that has not been examined for eye problems; it could be heartbreaking.

Progressive retinal atrophy (PRA) is quite serious but fortunately not very common. It is a degeneration of retinal visual cells that progresses to blindness. Unfortunately it often doesn't show up until the puppy is older, and some forms of PRA don't show up for several years. Electronic testing is expensive and often not easily available. Responsible breeders know the inheritance of PRA and check their breeding stock periodically to be sure it doesn't crop up. They try to identify the lines carrying the gene and either stay away from them or test breed to assure that the dogs they breed from are clear. Because of the seriousness of PRA, the Collie Club of America (CCA) Foundation funds research aimed at locating the genetic marker for this gene so that affected and carrier animals can be readily identified. They may now be very close to that goal.

CANINE HIP DYSPLASIA

Collies are usually listed as a low-incidence breed for hip dysplasia, but unfortunately they are also seldom x-rayed. From working with guide and service dogs where accurate hip information is imperative, I know that hip dysplasia is more common in Collies than breeders realize. Where possible, choose puppies from a background of examined dogs. X-rays can be submitted to the Orthopedic Foundation of America (OFA) for an OFA number identifying dogs with good hip ratings, and this OFA number and rating is generally proudly noted on pedigrees. Canine hip dysplasia (CHD) remains the most common orthopedic problem veterinarians encounter, and is considered a very complex disease controlled by a variety of genes.

MANGE

Demodectic mange, if localized to a few spots, develops in most breeds and spontaneously disappears. It usually results from stress to the puppy's immune system due to food changes, a new home, shots and teething. However, generalized mange has a genetic component often requiring more intensive treatment.

BLOAT (GASTRIC DILATION-VOLVULUS)

Collies are susceptible to this life-threatening disorder. Gastric dilation is a distention of the stomach. If the stomach twists on its axis, it is called gastric *volvulus*. Once the stomach twists, there is a rapid accumulation of gas that cannot escape and stomach tissue begins to die. Surrounding organs are displaced, followed by shock, infection, rupture of the stomach and death.

ACUTE PANCREATITIS

Acute pancreatitis often strikes spontaneously. Severe abdominal pain and vomiting are common symptoms. This disease, often unidentified until too late, is more prevalent in some breeds and families. Collies do appear susceptible. Usually victims are 7 or older, but it can occur in younger dogs. Overweight dogs are at risk.

> **NOT JUST FOR SUNBURN**
>
> Aloe vera is great for cuts and wounds. It contains the proven wound-healing ingredients allantoin and acemannan, which also stimulate tissue repair.

Spaying and Neutering

Most responsible breeders sell dogs on a spay or neuter contract, so hopefully this is something you have already thought about. This makes any dog a better pet, and a healthier one, too. Neutered animals focus on their human families and homes and are not distracted by seasonal breeding influences. I disagree with early neutering, and prefer to neuter around 9 months of age, after puppies have developed physically and mentally, and have set their own basic personalities. Neutered animals are less likely to roam, make fine watchdogs or children's' pets and are free of problems involved with unaltered breeding age animals.

Diarrhea and Vomiting

The Collie you love deserves a long, happy life. Be a responsible pet owner and spay or neuter your dog. You will both be happier.

Diarrhea and vomiting occur in healthy dogs from dietary upsets, sudden diet changes, stress, exertion or as early indications of a problem. If the dog seems otherwise normal, give a couple of Pepto-Bismol™ tablets; remove all food and water for awhile and watch him. If the dog appears depressed, take his temperature rectally; normal for a dog is 101.5° to 102°F. Beware of giving most "human" products as some dogs are intolerant to these medications and can have a bad reaction; others handle them fine. If the dog, particularly a puppy, seems lethargic, if the vomiting or diarrhea is projectile, has an unusual odor or if there is blood in the stool or vomit, alert your veterinarian and follow his advice. Look for anything the dog could have gotten into . . . many household and garden products are deadly for dogs.

Emergencies

In an emergency, what you do and how fast you do it literally may mean life or death to your Collie. Dogs often go where they shouldn't or get into harmful, even lethal substances. Accidents happen despite our best intentions. Planning ahead minimizes panic.

Know your veterinarian's phone number and how to reach him in an emergency. Also know your local poison control emergency number. Many areas have a pet emergency hospital; know its location and hours.

MUZZLING AND TRANSPORTING

Know some basic techniques of restraining and transporting a large, powerful dog. Even the sweetest Collie may bite from severe pain or fear. An effective temporary muzzle can be made of anything soft and strong that can be looped around a dog's muzzle and behind his head. Bring the loop under his chin and up around his muzzle, tying a half-knot. Bring the ends back down under the chin and tie a second half-knot, then bring the ends around the neck and tie securely behind the ears in a bow, allowing quick release as needed. Be sure it is tight enough so the dog cannot rub or pull it off, but allows for breathing.

Use a scarf or old hose to make a temporary muzzle, as shown.

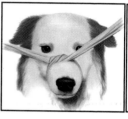

If your Collie must be carried, find a helper. A large towel or folded blanket can be used by placing the dog in the center and lifting by the edges. A large enough board, a folding table, a camp bed or folding patio lounger can all serve as a stretcher. Transporting this way is usually easier, safer and more comfortable for you and the dog than carrying him in your arms.

BLEEDING

To stop bleeding, apply a pressure bandage. Use strips of gauze if you have them, or any sturdy, clean material. Wrap the injured area if possible, applying even pressure. If the tissue below the wound swells, loosen the bandage. Where you can't wrap the wound, apply pressure directly on the wound with a clean cloth, or even your hand, to stem blood loss.

SHOCK

Shock often accompanies traumatic injury, and immediate action is vital if the dog shows these symptoms: rapid, weak heartbeat; dilated pupils; pale gums; and weakness. Do whatever is necessary, then immediately get the dog to a veterinarian; time is vital. Keep him quiet and warm, as shock victims often have low body temperatures. Shock can also occur after veterinary treatment, or during serious illness.

HEATSTROKE

Your Collie's normal body temperature is 101.5° to 102°F, so NEVER leave him in a hot car or pen him in a confined area in heat or sun. Always insure that he has good ventilation, shade and water during hot weather. It only takes a few minutes to send a dog into heatstroke. Signs of heatstroke are: rapid breathing with shallow breaths and rapid heartbeat. Take him immediately to your veterinarian. Heatstroke can cause internal damage.

POISONING

Know the type, amount and time your dog ingested poison. Some poisons are absorbed through the skin, so determine what he may have been exposed to. If you can't reach your vet, call the local or national poison control center. The National Animal Poison Control Center hot line is (800) 548-2423 ($30 per case) or (900) 680-0000 ($20 first five minutes; $2.95 each additional minute). Bring any containers or labels with you.

BURNS

For minor burns, clip away the hair, clean with a mild soap if necessary and use an antibiotic ointment. If the burn is more serious, the dog will need immediate emergency care.

DOG BITES

Puncture wounds from dog bites may not look too serious, but require immediate attention. The small visible bite area is no indication of the damage to muscles and tissue. Clean the wound thoroughly and flush it out with an antiseptic solution. It is best for a veterinarian to examine it; the dog may require an antibiotic shot if the wound is dirty.

The Aging Collie

Collies age at various rates depending on health, care and even genetics. Your dog will live approximately the lifespan of his parents. Eleven or 12 years of age is common, but some can be much older; several of ours have gone 15 to 17 years. Collies generally age with dignity and make wonderful senior citizens. Please keep up with dental attention and a yearly veterinary checkup. Watch for vision and hearing problems, and be more protective of his safety. Trim away unnecessary, unseen hair between the legs, under the armpits, to make grooming easier.

As he ages, your Collie will gradually slow down, but his senior years could be the best you will share together.

Elderly Collies, like elderly people, sleep more, nap at unusual times and show signs of slowing. They usually gray around the face, though in some lines this shows much earlier than in others. Make sure your aging Collie has a comfortable place to sleep, out of drafts, with thick, soft bedding. Follow the diet guidelines in chapter 5. Many geriatric problems can be managed. The older Collie will have more problems moving about, and you must plan ahead to make provisions for your dog.

SAYING GOODBYE

When through illness or discomfort it becomes obvious that you must make the decision, discuss euthanasia with your veterinarian so that you will understand how and when to respond. Allow the older dog to leave you with pride and dignity intact. Sometimes we love them too much and hold on past the time we should have let them go.

If children are involved, plan your explanation to them in advance. Do not just have the Collie chum disappear one day. Death, whether of a family member or a beloved pet, is traumatic for a child. Several books are available on the subject; when the time draws near, you might want to select one to help you plan.

When my daughter Katie was small, I helped her understand that her beloved Douglas was aging. As we petted and hugged the big black Collie, now nearly deaf and blind but so happy to be with us, and explained the physical changes going on, Katie held my hand and whispered, "But, Mom, he's still beautiful on the inside."

Perhaps this is what we should remember. Our dogs are with us such a short time and make such a lasting impression on our lives. We are so very, very blessed to have known them.

Your Happy, Healthy Pet

Your Dog's Name _____

Name on Your Dog's Pedigree (if your dog has one) _____

_____

Where Your Dog Came From _____

_____

Your Dog's Birthday _____

Your Dog's Veterinarian

    Name _____

    Address _____

    Phone Number_____

    Emergency Number_____

Your Dog's Health

    Vaccines

        type _____ date given _____

        type _____ date given _____

        type _____ date given _____

        type _____ date given _____

    Heartworm

        date tested _____ type used_____ start date _____

Your Dog's License Number_____

Groomer's Name and Number _____

Dogsitter/Walker's Name and Number_____

Awards Your Dog Has Won

    Award _____ date earned _____

    Award _____ date earned _____

part three

Enjoying your Dog

chapter 8

Basic
Training

by Ian Dunbar, Ph.D., MRCVS

Training is the jewel in the crown—the most important aspect of doggy husbandry. There is no more important variable influencing dog behavior and temperament than the dog's education: A well-trained, well-behaved and good-natured puppydog is always a joy to live with, but an untrained and uncivilized dog can be a perpetual nightmare. Moreover, deny the dog an education and she will not have the opportunity to fulfill her own canine potential; neither will she have the ability to communicate effectively with her human companions.

Luckily, modern psychological training methods are easy, efficient, effective and, above all, considerably dog-friendly and user-friendly.

Doggy education is as simple as it is enjoyable. But before you can have a good time play-training with your new dog, you have to learn what to do and how to do it. There is no bigger variable influencing the success of dog training than the *owner's* experience and expertise. *Before you embark on the dog's education, you must first educate yourself.*

Basic Training for Owners

Ideally, basic owner training should begin well *before* you select your dog. Find out all you can about your chosen breed first, then master rudimentary training and handling skills. If you already have your puppy-dog, owner training is a dire emergency—the clock is ticking! Especially for puppies, the first few weeks at home are the most important and influential days in the dog's life. Indeed, the cause of most adolescent and adult problems may be traced back to the initial days the pup explores her new home. This is the time to establish the *status quo*—to teach the puppydog how you would like her to behave and so prevent otherwise quite predictable problems.

In addition to consulting breeders and breed books such as this one (which understandably have a positive breed bias), seek out as many pet owners with your breed as you can find. Good points are obvious. What you want to find out are the breed-specific *problems*, so you can nip them in the bud. In particular, you should talk to owners with *adolescent* dogs and make a list of all anticipated problems. Most important, *test drive* at least half a dozen adolescent and adult dogs of your breed yourself. An 8-week-old puppy is deceptively easy to handle, but she will acquire adult size, speed and strength in just four months, so you should learn now what to prepare for.

Puppy and pet dog training classes offer a convenient venue to locate pet owners and observe dogs in action. For a list of suitable trainers in your area, contact the Association of Pet Dog Trainers (see chapter 13). You may also begin your basic owner training by observing

other owners in class. Watch as many classes and test
drive as many dogs as possible. Select an upbeat, dog-
friendly, people-friendly, fun-and-games, puppydog pet
training class to learn the ropes. Also, watch training
videos and read training books. You must find out what
to do and how to do it *before* you have to do it.

Principles of Training

Most people think training comprises teaching the dog
to do things such as sit, speak and roll over, but even a
4-week-old pup knows how to do these things already.
Instead, the first step in training involves teaching
the dog human words for each dog behavior and activity and for each aspect of the dog's environment. That
way you, the owner, can more easily participate in the
dog's domestic education by directing her to perform
specific actions appropriately, that is, at the right time,
in the right place and so on. Training opens communication channels, enabling an educated dog to at least
understand her owner's requests.

In addition to teaching a dog *what* we want her to
do, it is also necessary to teach her *why* she should do
what we ask. Indeed, 95 percent of training revolves
around motivating the dog *to want to do* what we want.
Dogs often understand what their owners want; they
just don't see the point of doing it—especially when
the owner's repetitively boring and seemingly senseless
instructions are totally at odds with much more press-
ing and exciting doggy distractions. It is not so much
the dog that is being stubborn or dominant; rather, it
is the owner who has failed to acknowledge the dog's
needs and feelings and to approach training from the
dog's point of view.

THE MEANING OF INSTRUCTIONS

The secret to successful training is learning how to use
training lures to predict or prompt specific behaviors—
to coax the dog to do what you want *when* you want.
Any highly valued object (such as a treat or toy) may be
used as a lure, which the dog will follow with her eyes

and nose. Moving the lure in specific ways entices the dog to move her nose, head and entire body in specific ways. In fact, by learning the art of manipulating various lures, it is possible to teach the dog to assume virtually any body position and perform any action. Once you have control over the expression of the dog's behaviors and can elicit any body position or behavior at will, you can easily teach the dog to perform on request.

Teach your dog words for each activity she needs to know, like down.

Tell your dog what you want her to do, use a lure to entice her to respond correctly, then profusely praise and maybe reward her once she performs the desired action. For example, verbally request "Tina, sit!" while you move a squeaky toy upwards and backwards over the dog's muzzle (lure-movement and hand signal), smile knowingly as she looks up (to follow the lure) and sits down (as a result of canine anatomical engineering), then praise her to distraction ("Gooood Tina!"). Squeak the toy, offer a training treat and give your dog and yourself a pat on the back.

Being able to elicit desired responses over and over enables the owner to reward the dog over and over. Consequently, the dog begins to think training is fun. For example, the more the dog is rewarded for sitting, the more she enjoys sitting. Eventually the dog comes to realize that, whereas most sitting is appreciated, sitting immediately upon request usually prompts especially enthusiastic praise and a slew of high-level rewards. The dog begins to sit on cue much of the time, showing that she is starting to grasp the meaning of the owner's verbal request and hand signal.

WHY COMPLY?

Most dogs enjoy initial lure-reward training and are only too happy to comply with their owners' wishes. Unfortunately, repetitive drilling without appreciative feedback tends to diminish the dog's enthusiasm until she eventually fails to see the point of complying anymore. Moreover, as the dog approaches adolescence she becomes more easily distracted as she develops other interests. Lengthy sessions with repetitive exercises tend to bore and demotivate both parties. If it's not fun, the owner doesn't do it and neither does the dog.

Integrate training into your dog's life: The greater number of training sessions each day and the *shorter* they are, the more willingly compliant your dog will

become. Make sure to have a short (just a few seconds) training interlude before every enjoyable canine activity. For example, ask your dog to sit to greet people, to sit before you throw her Frisbee and to sit for her supper. Really, sitting is no different from a canine "Please."

To train your dog, you need gentle hands, a loving heart and a good attitude.

Also, include numerous short training interludes during every enjoyable canine pastime, for example, when playing with the dog or when she is running in the park. In this fashion, doggy distractions may be effectively converted into rewards for training. Just as all games have rules, fun becomes training . . . and training becomes fun.

Eventually, rewards actually become unnecessary to continue motivating your dog. If trained with consideration and kindness, performing the desired behaviors will become self-rewarding and, in a sense, your dog will motivate herself. Just as it is not necessary to reward a human companion during an enjoyable walk in the park, or following a game of tennis, it is hardly necessary to reward our best friend—the dog—for walking by our side or while playing fetch. Human company during enjoyable activities is reward enough for most dogs.

Even though your dog has become self-motivating, it's still good to praise and pet her a lot and offer rewards once in a while, especially for a good job well done. And if for no other reason, praising and rewarding others is good for the human heart.

PUNISHMENT

Without a doubt, lure-reward training is by far the best way to teach: Entice your dog to do what you want and then reward her for doing so. Unfortunately, a human shortcoming is to take the good for granted and to moan and groan at the bad. Specifically, the dog's many good behaviors are ignored while the owner focuses on punishing the dog for making mistakes. In extreme cases, instruction is *limited* to punishing mistakes made by a trainee dog, child, employee or husband, even though it has been proven punishment training is notoriously inefficient and ineffective and is decidedly unfriendly and combative. It teaches the dog that training is a drag, almost as quickly as it teaches the dog to dislike her trainer. Why treat our best friends like our worst enemies?

Punishment training is also much more laborious and time consuming. Whereas it takes only a finite amount of time to teach a dog what to chew, for example, it takes much, much longer to punish the dog for each and every mistake. Remember, *there is only one right way!* So why not teach that right way from the outset?!

To make matters worse, punishment training causes severe lapses in the dog's reliability. Since it is obviously impossible to punish the dog each and every time she misbehaves, the dog quickly learns to distinguish between those times when she must comply (so as to avoid impending punishment) and those times when she need not comply, because punishment is impossible. Such times include when the dog is off leash and 6 feet away, when the owner is otherwise engaged (talking to a friend, watching television, taking a shower, tending to the baby or chatting on the telephone) or when the dog is left at home alone.

Instances of misbehavior will be numerous when the owner is away, because even when the dog complied in the owner's looming presence, she did so unwillingly. The dog was forced to act against her will, rather than molding her will to want to please. Hence, when the owner is absent, not only does the dog know she need not comply, she simply does not want to. Again, the trainee is not a stubborn vindictive beast, but rather the trainer has failed to teach. Punishment training invariably creates unpredictable Jekyll and Hyde behavior.

Trainer's Tools

Many training books extol the virtues of a vast array of training paraphernalia and electronic and metallic gizmos, most of which are designed for canine restraint, correction and punishment, rather than for actual facilitation of doggy education. In reality, most effective training tools are not found in stores; they come from within ourselves. In addition to a willing dog, all you really need is a functional human brain, gentle hands, a loving heart and a good attitude.

In terms of equipment, all dogs do require a quality buckle collar to sport dog tags and to attach the leash (for safety and to comply with local leash laws). Hollow chew toys (like Kongs or sterilized longbones) and a dog bed or collapsible crate are musts for housetraining. Three additional tools are required:

1. specific lures (training treats and toys) to predict and prompt specific desired behaviors;

2. rewards (praise, affection, training treats and toys) to reinforce for the dog what a lot of fun it all is; and

3. knowledge—how to convert the dog's favorite activities and games (potential distractions to training) into "life-rewards," which may be employed to facilitate training.

The most powerful of these is *knowledge*. Education is the key! Watch training classes, participate in training classes, watch videos, read books, enjoy play-training with your dog and then your dog will say "Please," and your dog will say "Thank you!"

Housetraining

If dogs were left to their own devices, certainly they would chew, dig and bark for entertainment and then no doubt highlight a few areas of their living space with sprinkles of urine, in much the same way we decorate by hanging pictures. Consequently, when we ask a dog to live with us, we must teach her *where* she may dig, *where* she may perform her toilet duties, *what* she may chew and *when* she may bark. After all, when left at home alone for many hours, we cannot expect the dog to amuse herself by completing crosswords or watching the soaps on TV!

Also, it would be decidedly unfair to keep the house rules a secret from the dog, and then get angry and punish the poor critter for inevitably transgressing rules she did not even know existed. Remember: Without adequate education and guidance, the dog will be forced to establish her own rules—doggy rules—and most probably will be at odds with the owner's view of domestic living.

Since most problems develop during the first few days the dog is at home, prospective dog owners must be certain they are quite clear about the principles of housetraining *before* they get a dog. Early misbehaviors quickly become established as the *status quo*—

becoming firmly entrenched as hard-to-break bad habits, which set the precedent for years to come. Make sure to teach your dog good habits right from the start. Good habits are just as hard to break as bad ones!

Ideally, when a new dog comes home, try to arrange for someone to be present as much as possible during the first few days (for adult dogs) or weeks for puppies. With only a little forethought, it is surprisingly easy to find a puppy sitter, such as a retired person, who would be willing to eat from your refrigerator and watch your television while keeping an eye on the newcomer to encourage the dog to play with chew toys and to ensure she goes outside on a regular basis.

POTTY TRAINING

To teach the dog where to relieve herself:

1. never let her make a single mistake;

2. let her know where you want her to go; and

3. handsomely reward her for doing so: "GOOOOOOOD DOG!!!" liver treat, liver treat, liver treat!

Preventing Mistakes

A single mistake is a training disaster, since it heralds many more in future weeks. And each time the dog soils the house, this further reinforces the dog's unfortunate preference for an indoor, carpeted toilet. *Do not let an unhousetrained dog have full run of the house.*

When you are away from home, or cannot pay full attention, confine the dog to an area where elimination is appropriate, such as an outdoor run or, better still, a small, comfortable indoor kennel with access to an outdoor run. When confined in this manner, most dogs will naturally housetrain themselves.

If that's not possible, confine the dog to an area, such as a utility room, kitchen, basement or garage, where elimination may not be desired in the long run but as an interim measure it is certainly preferable to doing it all around the house. Use newspaper to cover the floor of the dog's day room. The newspaper may be used to soak up the urine and to wrap up and dispose of the feces. Once your dog develops a preferred spot for eliminating, it is only necessary to cover

that part of the floor with newspaper. The smaller papered area may then be moved (only a little each day) towards the door to the outside. Thus the dog will develop the tendency to go to the door when she needs to relieve herself.

Never confine an unhousetrained dog to a crate for long periods. Doing so would force the dog to soil the crate and ruin its usefulness as an aid for housetraining (see the following discussion).

Teaching Where

In order to teach your dog where you would like her to do her business, you have to be there to direct the proceedings—an obvious, yet often neglected, fact of life. In order to be there to teach the dog *where* to go, you need to know *when* she needs to go. Indeed, the success of housetraining depends on the owner's ability to predict these times. Certainly, a regular feeding schedule will facilitate prediction somewhat, but there is nothing like "loading the deck" and influencing the timing of the outcome yourself!

The first few weeks at home are the most important and influential in your dog's life.

Whenever you are at home, make sure the dog is under constant supervision and/or confined to a small

107

area. If already well trained, simply instruct the dog to lie down in her bed or basket. Alternatively, confine the dog to a crate (doggy den) or tie-down (a short, 18-inch lead that can be clipped to an eye hook in the baseboard near her bed). Short-term close confinement strongly inhibits urination and defecation, since the dog does not want to soil her sleeping area. Thus, when you release the puppydog each hour, she will definitely need to urinate immediately and defecate every third or fourth hour. Keep the dog confined to her doggy den and take her to her intended toilet area each hour, every hour and on the hour.

When taking your dog outside, instruct her to sit quietly before opening the door—she will soon learn to sit by the door when she needs to go out!

Teaching Why

Being able to predict when the dog needs to go enables the owner to be on the spot to praise and reward the dog. Each hour, hurry the dog to the intended toilet area in the yard, issue the appropriate instruction ("Go pee!" or "Go poop!"), then give the dog three to four minutes to produce. Praise and offer a couple of training treats when successful. The treats are important because many people fail to praise their dogs with feeling . . . and housetraining is hardly the time for understatement. So either loosen up and enthusiastically praise that dog: "Wuzzzer-wuzzer-wuzzer, hooooser good wuffer den? Hoooo went pee for Daddy?" Or say "Good dog!" as best you can and offer the treats for effect.

Following elimination is an ideal time for a spot of play-training in the yard or house. Also, an empty dog may be allowed greater freedom around the house for the next half hour or so, just as long as you keep an eye out to make sure she does not get into other kinds of mischief. If you are preoccupied and cannot pay full attention, confine the dog to her doggy den once more to enjoy a peaceful snooze or to play with her many chew toys.

If your dog does not eliminate within the allotted time outside—no biggie! Back to her doggy den, and then try again after another hour.

As I own large dogs, I always feel more relaxed walking an empty dog, knowing that I will not need to finish our stroll weighted down with bags of feces!

Beware of falling into the trap of walking the dog to get her to eliminate. The good ol' dog walk is such an enormous highlight in the dog's life that it represents the single biggest potential reward in domestic dogdom. However, when in a hurry, or during inclement weather, many owners abruptly terminate the walk the moment the dog has done her business. This, in effect, severely punishes the dog for doing the right thing, in the right place at the right time. Consequently, many dogs become strongly inhibited from eliminating outdoors because they know it will signal an abrupt end to an otherwise thoroughly enjoyable walk.

Instead, instruct the dog to relieve herself in the yard prior to going for a walk. If you follow the above instructions, most dogs soon learn to eliminate on cue. As soon as the dog eliminates, praise (and offer a treat or two)—"Good dog! Let's go walkies!" Use the walk as a reward for eliminating in the yard. If the dog does not go, put her back in her doggy den and think about a walk later on. You will find with a "No feces—no walk" policy, your dog will become one of the fastest defecators in the business.

If you do not have a backyard, instruct the dog to eliminate right outside your front door prior to the walk. Not only will this facilitate clean up and disposal of the feces in your own trash can but, also, the walk may again be used as a colossal reward.

CHEWING AND BARKING

Short-term close confinement also teaches the dog that occasional quiet moments are a reality of domestic living. Your puppydog is extremely impressionable during her first few weeks at home. Regular confinement at this time soon exerts a calming influence over the dog's personality. Remember, once the dog is housetrained and calmer, there will be a whole lifetime ahead for the dog to enjoy full run of the house and garden. On the other hand, by letting the newcomer have unrestricted access to the entire household and allowing her to run willy-nilly, she will most certainly develop a bunch of behavior problems in short order, no doubt necessitating confinement later in life. It would not be fair to remedially restrain and confine a dog you have trained, through neglect, to run free.

When confining the dog, make sure she always has an impressive array of suitable chew toys. Kongs and sterilized longbones (both readily available from pet stores) make the best chew toys, since they are hollow and may be stuffed with treats to heighten the dog's interest. For example, by stuffing the little hole at the top of a Kong with a small piece of freeze-dried liver, the dog will not want to leave it alone.

Remember, treats do not have to be junk food and they certainly should not represent extra calories. Rather, treats should be part of each dog's regular daily diet: Some food may be served in the dog's bowl for breakfast and dinner, some food may be used as training treats, and some food may be used for stuffing chew toys. I regularly stuff my dogs' many Kongs with different shaped biscuits and kibble.

Make sure your puppy has suitable chew toys.

The kibble seems to fall out fairly easily, as do the oval-shaped biscuits, thus rewarding the dog instantaneously for checking out the chew toys. The bone-shaped biscuits fall out after a while, rewarding the dog for worrying at the chew toy. But the triangular biscuits never come out. They remain inside the Kong as lures, maintaining the dog's fascination with her chew toy. To further focus the dog's interest, I always make sure to flavor the triangular biscuits by rubbing them with a little cheese or freeze-dried liver.

To teach come, call your dog, open your arms as a welcoming signal, wave a toy or a treat and praise for every step in your direction.

If stuffed chew toys are reserved especially for times the dog is confined, the puppydog will soon learn to enjoy quiet moments in her doggy den and she will quickly develop a chew-toy habit— a good habit! This is a simple *autoshaping* process; all the owner has to do is set up the situation and the dog all but trains herself— easy and effective. Even when the dog is given run of the house, her first inclination will be to indulge her rewarding chew-toy habit rather than destroy less-attractive household articles, such as curtains, carpets, chairs and compact disks. Similarly, a chew-toy chewer will be less inclined to scratch and chew herself excessively. Also, if the dog busies herself as a recreational chewer, she will be less inclined to develop into a recreational barker or digger when left at home alone.

Stuff a number of chew toys whenever the dog is left confined and remove the extra-special-tasting treats when you return. Your dog will now amuse herself with her chew toys before falling asleep and then resume playing with her chew toys when she expects you to return. Since most owner-absent misbehavior happens right after you leave and right before your expected return, your puppydog will now be conveniently preoccupied with her chew toys at these times.

Come and Sit

Most puppies will happily approach virtually anyone, whether called or not; that is, until they collide with adolescence and

develop other more important doggy interests, such as sniffing a multiplicity of exquisite odors on the grass. Your mission, Mr./Ms. Owner, is to teach and reward the pup for coming reliably, willingly and happily when called—and you have just three months to get it done. Unless adequately reinforced, your puppy's tendency to approach people will self-destruct by adolescence.

Call your dog ("Tina, come!"), open your arms (and maybe squat down) as a welcoming signal, waggle a treat or toy as a lure and reward the puppydog when she comes running. Do not wait to praise the dog until she reaches you—she may come 95 percent of the way and then run off after some distraction. Instead, praise the dog's *first* step towards you and continue praising enthusiastically for *every* step she takes in your direction.

When the rapidly approaching puppy dog is three lengths away from impact, instruct her to sit ("Tina, sit!") and hold the lure in front of you in an outstretched hand to prevent her from hitting you midchest and knocking you flat on your back! As Tina decelerates to nose the lure, move the treat upwards and backwards just over her muzzle with an upwards motion of your extended arm (palm-upwards). As the dog looks up to follow the lure, she will sit down (if she jumps up, you are holding the lure too high). Praise the dog for sitting. Move backwards and call her again. Repeat this many times over, always praising when Tina comes and sits; on occasion, reward her.

For the first couple of trials, use a training treat both as a lure to entice the dog to come and sit and as a reward for doing so. Thereafter, try to use different items as lures and rewards. For example, lure the dog with a Kong or Frisbee but reward her with a food treat. Or lure the dog with a food treat but pat her and throw a tennis ball as a reward. After just a few repetitions, dispense with the lures and rewards; the dog will begin to respond willingly to your verbal requests and hand signals just for the prospect of praise from your heart and affection from your hands.

Instruct every family member, friend and visitor how to get the dog to come and sit. Invite people over for a series of pooch parties; do not keep the pup a secret— let other people enjoy this puppy, and let the pup enjoy other people. Puppydog parties are not only fun, they easily attract a lot of people to help *you* train *your* dog. Unless you teach your dog how to meet people, that is, to sit for greetings, no doubt the dog will resort to jumping up. Then you and the visitors will get annoyed, and the dog will be punished. This is not fair. *Send out those invitations for puppy parties and teach your dog to be mannerly and socially acceptable.*

Even though your dog quickly masters obedient recalls in the house, her reliability may falter when playing in the backyard or local park. Ironically, it is *the owner* who has unintentionally trained the dog *not* to respond in these instances. By allowing the dog to play and run around and otherwise have a good time, but then to call the dog to put her on leash to take her home, the dog quickly learns playing is fun but training is a drag. Thus, playing in the park becomes a severe distraction, which works against training. Bad news!

Instead, whether playing with the dog off leash or on leash, request her to come at frequent intervals—say, every minute or so. On most occasions, praise and pet the dog for a few seconds while she is sitting, then tell her to go play again. For especially fast recalls, offer a couple of training treats and take the time to praise and pet the dog enthusiastically before releasing her. The dog will learn that coming when called is not necessarily the end of the play session, and neither is it the end of the world; rather, it signals an enjoyable, quality time-out with the owner before resuming play once more. In fact, playing in the park now becomes a very effective life-reward, which works to facilitate training by reinforcing each obedient and timely recall. Good news!

Sit, Down, Stand and Rollover

Teaching the dog a variety of body positions is easy for owner and dog, impressive for spectators and

113

extremely useful for all. Using lure-reward techniques, it is possible to train several positions at once to verbal commands or hand signals (which impress the socks off onlookers).

Sit and **down**—the two control commands—prevent or resolve nearly a hundred behavior problems. For example, if the dog happily and obediently sits or lies down when requested, she cannot jump on visitors, dash out the front door, run around and chase her tail, pester other dogs, harass cats or annoy family, friends or strangers. Additionally, "Sit" or "Down" are the best emergency commands for off-leash control.

It is easier to teach and maintain a reliable sit than maintain a reliable recall. *Sit* is the purest and simplest of commands—either the dog is sitting or she is not. If there is any change of circumstances or potential danger in the park, for example, simply instruct the dog to sit. If she sits, you have a number of options: Allow the dog to resume playing when she is safe, walk up and put the dog on leash or call the dog. The dog will be much more likely to come when called if she has already acknowledged her compliance by sitting. If the dog does not sit in the park—train her to!

Stand and *rollover-stay* are the two positions for examining the dog. Your veterinarian will love you to distraction if you take a little time to teach the dog to stand still and roll over and play possum. Also, your vet bills will be smaller because it will take the veterinarian less time to examine your dog. The rollover-stay is an especially useful command and is really just a variation of the down-stay: Whereas the dog lies prone in the traditional down, she lies supine in the rollover-stay.

As with teaching come and sit, the training techniques to teach the dog to assume all other body positions on cue are user-friendly and dog-friendly. Simply give the appropriate request, lure the dog into the desired body position using a training treat or toy and then *praise* (and maybe reward) the dog as soon as she complies. Try not to touch the dog to get her to respond. If you teach the dog by guiding her into position, the dog will quickly learn that rump-pressure means sit, for example, but as yet you still have no control over your dog if she is just 6 feet away. It will still be necessary to teach the dog to sit on request. So do not make training a time-consuming two-step process; instead, teach the dog to sit to a verbal request or hand signal from the outset. Once the dog sits willingly when requested, by all means use your hands to pet the dog when she does so.

To teach **down** when the dog is already sitting, say "Tina, down!," hold the lure in one hand (palm down) and lower that hand to the floor between the dog's forepaws. As the dog lowers her head to follow the lure, slowly move the lure away from the dog just a fraction (in front of her paws). The dog will lie down as she stretches her nose forward to follow the lure. Praise the dog when she does so. If the dog stands up, you pulled the lure away too far and too quickly.

When teaching the dog to lie down from the standing position, say "Down" and lower the lure to the floor as before. Once the dog has lowered her forequarters and assumed a play bow, gently and slowly move the lure *towards* the dog between her forelegs. Praise the dog as soon as her rear end plops down.

After just a couple of trials it will be possible to alternate sits and downs and have the dog energetically perform doggy push-ups. Praise the dog a lot, and after half a dozen or so push-ups reward the dog with a training treat or toy. You will notice the more energetically you move your arm—upwards (palm up) to get the dog to sit, and downwards (palm down) to get the dog to lie down—the more energetically the dog responds to your requests. Now try training the dog in silence and you will notice she has also learned to respond to hand signals. Yeah! Not too shabby for the first session.

To teach **stand** from the sitting position, say "Tina, stand," slowly move the lure half a dog-length away from the dog's nose, keeping it at nose level, and praise the dog as she stands to follow the lure. As soon

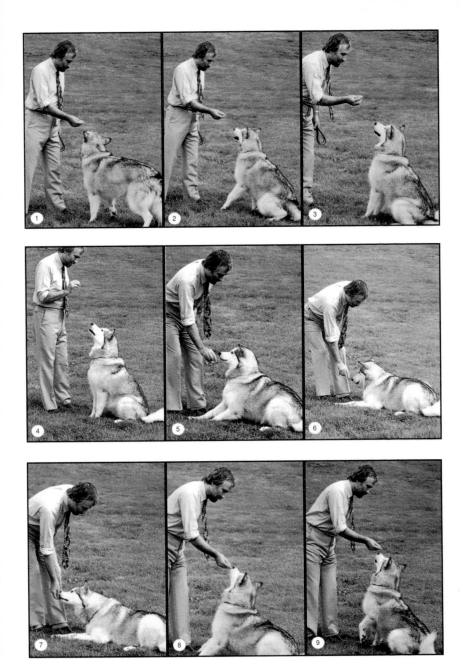

Using a food lure to teach sit, down and stand. 1) "Phoenix, sit." 2) Hand palm upwards, move lure up and back over dog's muzzle. 3) "Good sit, Phoenix!" 4) "Phoenix, down." 5) Hand palm downwards, move lure down to lie between dog's forepaws. 6) "Phoenix, off. Good down, Phoenix!" 7) "Phoenix, sit!" 8) Palm upwards, move lure up and back, keeping it close to dog's muzzle. 9) "Good sit, Phoenix!"

10) "Phoenix, stand!" 11) Move lure away from dog at nose height, then lower it a tad. 12) "Phoenix, off! Good stand, Phoenix!" 13) "Phoenix, down!" 14) Hand palm downwards, move lure down to lie between dog's forepaws. 15) "Phoenix, off! Good down-stay, Phoenix!" 16) "Phoenix, stand!" 17) Move lure away from dog's muzzle up to nose height. 18) "Phoenix, off! Good stand-stay, Phoenix. Now we'll make the vet and groomer happy!"

as the dog stands, lower the lure to just beneath the dog's chin to entice her to look down; otherwise she will stand and then sit immediately. To prompt the dog to stand from the down position, move the lure half a dog-length upwards and away from the dog, holding the lure at standing nose height from the floor.

Teaching **rollover** is best started from the down position, with the dog lying on one side, or at least with both hind legs stretched out on the same side. Say "Tina, bang!" and move the lure backwards and alongside the dog's muzzle to her elbow (on the side of her outstretched hind legs). Once the dog looks to the side and backwards, very slowly move the lure upwards to the dog's shoulder and backbone. Tickling the dog in the goolies (groin area) often invokes a reflex-raising of the hind leg as an appeasement gesture, which facilitates the tendency to roll over. If you move the lure too quickly and the dog jumps into the standing position, have patience and start again. As soon as the dog rolls onto her back, keep the lure stationary and mesmerize the dog with a relaxing tummy rub.

To teach **rollover-stay** when the dog is standing or moving, say "Tina, bang!" and give the appropriate hand signal (with index finger pointed and thumb cocked in true Sam Spade fashion), then in one fluid movement lure her to first lie down and then rollover-stay as above.

Teaching the dog to **stay** in each of the above four positions becomes a piece of cake after first teaching the dog not to worry at the toy or treat training lure. This is best accomplished by hand feeding dinner kibble. Hold a piece of kibble firmly in your hand and softly instruct "Off!" Ignore any licking and slobbering *for however long the dog worries at the treat,* but say "Take it!" and offer the kibble *the instant* the dog breaks contact with her muzzle. Repeat this a few times, and then up the ante and insist the dog remove her muzzle for one whole second before offering the kibble. Then progressively refine your criteria and have the dog not touch your hand (or treat) for longer and longer periods on each trial, such as for two seconds, four seconds, then six, ten, fifteen, twenty, thirty seconds and so on.

The dog soon learns: (1) worrying at the treat never gets results, whereas (2) noncontact is often rewarded after a variable time lapse.

Teaching *"Off!"* has many useful applications in its own right. Additionally, instructing the dog not to touch a training lure often produces spontaneous and magical stays. Request the dog to stand-stay, for example, and not to touch the lure. At first set your sights on a short two-second stay before rewarding the dog. (Remember, every long journey begins with a single step.) However, on subsequent trials, gradually and progressively increase the length of stay required to receive a reward. In no time at all your dog will stand calmly for a minute or so.

Relevancy Training

Once you have taught the dog what you expect her to do when requested to come, sit, lie down, stand, rollover and stay, the time is right to teach the dog *why* she should comply with your wishes. The secret is to have many (*many*) extremely short training interludes (two to five seconds each) at numerous (*numerous*) times during the course of the dog's day. Especially work with the dog immediately *before* the dog's good times and *during* the dog's good times. For example, ask your dog to sit and/or lie down each time before opening doors, serving meals, offering treats and tummy rubs; ask the dog to perform a few controlled doggy push-ups before letting her off leash or throwing a tennis ball; and perhaps request the dog to sit-down-sit-stand-down-stand-rollover before inviting her to cuddle on the couch.

Similarly, request the dog to sit many times during play or on walks, and in no time at all the dog will be only too pleased to follow your instructions because she has learned that a compliant response heralds all sorts of goodies. Basically all you are trying to teach the dog is how to say please: "Please throw the tennis ball. Please may I snuggle on the couch."

Remember, it is important to keep training interludes short and to have many short sessions each and every day. The shortest (and most useful) session comprises asking the dog to sit and then go play during a play session. When trained this way, your dog will soon associate training with good times. In fact, the dog may be unable to distinguish between training and good times and, indeed, there should be no distinction. The warped concept that training involves forcing the dog to comply and/or dominating her will is totally at odds with the picture of a truly well-trained dog. In reality, enjoying a game of training with a dog is no different from enjoying a game of backgammon or tennis with a friend; and walking with a dog should be no different from strolling with a spouse, or with buddies on the golf course.

Walk by Your Side

Many people attempt to teach a dog to heel by putting her on a leash and physically correcting the dog when she makes mistakes. There are a number of things seriously wrong with this approach, the first being that most people do not want precision heeling; rather, they simply want the dog to follow or walk by their side. Second, when physically restrained during "training," even though the dog may grudgingly mope by your side when "handcuffed" on leash, let's see what happens when she is off leash. History! The dog is in the next county because she never enjoyed walking with you on leash and you have no control over her off leash. So let's just teach the dog off leash from the outset to *want* to walk with us. Third, if the dog has not been trained to heel, it is a trifle hasty to think about punishing the poor dog for making mistakes and breaking heeling rules she didn't even know existed. This is simply not fair! Surely, if the dog had been adequately taught how to heel, she would seldom make mistakes and hence there would be no need to correct the dog. Remember, each mistake and each correction (punishment) advertise the trainer's inadequacy, not the dog's. The dog is not stubborn, she is not stupid and she is not bad. Even if she were, she would still require training, so let's train her properly.

Let's teach the dog to *enjoy* following us and to *want* to walk by our side off leash. Then it will be easier to teach high-precision off-leash heeling patterns if desired. Before going on outdoor walks, it is necessary to teach the dog not to pull. Then it becomes easy to teach on-leash walking and heeling because the dog already wants to walk with you, she is familiar with the desired walking and heeling positions and she knows not to pull.

FOLLOWING

Start by training your dog to follow you. Many puppies will follow if you simply walk away from them and maybe click your fingers or chuckle. Adult dogs may require additional enticement to stimulate them to follow, such as a training lure or, at the very least, a lively trainer. To teach the dog to follow: (1) keep walking and (2) walk away from the dog. If the dog attempts to lead or lag, change pace; slow down if the dog forges too far ahead, but speed up if she lags too far behind. Say "Steady!" or "Easy!" each time before you slow down and "Quickly!" or "Hustle!" each time before you speed up, and the dog will learn to change pace on cue. If the dog lags or leads too far, or if she wanders right or left, simply walk quickly in the opposite direction and maybe even run away from the dog and hide.

Practicing is a lot of fun; you can set up a course in your home, yard or park to do this. Indoors, entice the dog to follow upstairs, into a bedroom, into the bathroom, downstairs, around the living room couch, zigzagging between dining room chairs and into the kitchen for dinner. Outdoors, get the dog to follow around park benches, trees, shrubs and along walkways and lines in the grass. (For safety outdoors, it is advisable to attach a long line on the dog, but never exert corrective tension on the line.)

Remember, following has a lot to do with attitude—
your attitude! Most probably your dog will *not* want to
follow Mr. Grumpy Troll with the personality of wilted
lettuce. Lighten up—walk with a jaunty step, whistle a
happy tune, sing, skip and tell jokes to your dog and
she will be right there by your side.

BY YOUR SIDE

It is smart to train the dog to walk close on one side or
the other—either side will do, your choice. When walking, jogging or cycling, it is generally bad news to have
the dog suddenly cut in front of you. In fact, I train my
dogs to walk "By my side" and "Other side"—both very
useful instructions. It is possible to position the dog
fairly accurately by looking to the appropriate side and
clicking your fingers or slapping your thigh on that
side. A precise positioning may be attained by holding
a training lure, such as a chew toy, tennis ball or food
treat. Stop and stand still several times throughout the
walk, just as you would when window shopping or
meeting a friend. Use the lure to make sure the dog
slows down and stays close whenever you stop.

When teaching the dog to heel, we generally want
her to sit in heel position when we stop. Teach heel

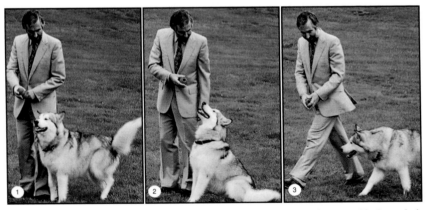

*Using a toy to teach sit-heel-sit sequences: 1) "Phoenix, sit!" Standing still, move lure up and back over dog's
muzzle . . . 2) to position dog sitting in heel position on your left side. 3) Say "Phoenix, heel!" and walk ahead,
wagging lure in left hand. Change lure to right hand in preparation for sit signal. Say "Sit" and then . . .*

122

position at the standstill and the dog will learn that the default heel position is sitting by your side (left or right—your choice, unless you wish to compete in obedience trials, in which case the dog must heel on the left).

Several times a day, stand up and call your dog to come and sit in heel position—"Tina, heel!" For example, instruct the dog to come to heel each time there are commercials on TV, or each time you turn a page of a novel, and the dog will get it in a single evening.

Practice straight-line heeling and turns separately. With the dog sitting at heel, teach her to turn in place. After each quarter-turn, half-turn or full turn in place, lure the dog to sit at heel. Now it's time for short straight-line heeling sequences, no more than a few steps at a time. Always think of heeling in terms of sit-heel-sit sequences—start and end with the dog in position and do your best to keep her there when moving. Progressively increase the number of steps in each sequence. When the dog remains close for 20 yards of straight-line heeling, it is time to add a few turns and then sign up for a happy-heeling obedience class to get some advice from the experts.

4) use hand signal to lure dog to sit as you stop. Eventually, dog will sit automatically at heel whenever you stop. 5) "Good dog!"

No Pulling on Leash

You can start teaching your dog not to pull on leash anywhere—in front of the television or outdoors—but regardless of location, you must not take a single step with tension in the leash. For a reason known only to dogs, even just a couple of paces of pulling on leash is intrinsically motivating and diabolically rewarding. Instead, attach the leash to the dog's collar, grasp the other end firmly with both hands held close to your chest, and stand still—do not budge an inch. Have somebody watch you with a stopwatch to time your progress, or else you will never believe this will work and so you will not even try the exercise, and your shoulder and the dog's neck will be traumatized for years to come.

Stand still and wait for the dog to stop pulling, and to sit and/or lie down. All dogs stop pulling and sit eventually. Most take only a couple of minutes; the all-time record is 22½ minutes. Time how long it takes. Gently praise the dog when she stops pulling, and as soon as she sits, enthusiastically praise the dog and take just one step forward, then immediately stand still. This single step usually demonstrates the ballistic reinforcing nature of pulling on leash; most dogs explode to the end of the leash, so be prepared for the strain. Stand firm and wait for the dog to sit again. Repeat this half a dozen times and you will probably notice a progressive reduction in the force of the dog's one-step explosions and a radical reduction in the time it takes for the dog to sit each time.

As the dog learns "Sit we go" and "Pull we stop," she will begin to walk forward calmly with each single step and automatically sit when you stop. Now try two steps before you stop. Wooooooo! Scary! When the dog has mastered two steps at a time, try for three. After each success, progressively increase the number of steps in the sequence: try four steps and then six, eight, ten and twenty steps before stopping. Congratulations! You are now walking the dog on leash.

Whenever walking with the dog (off leash or on leash), make sure you stop periodically to practice a few position commands and stays before instructing the dog to "Walk on!" (Remember, you want the dog to be compliant everywhere, not just in the kitchen when her dinner is at hand.) For example, stopping every 25 yards to briefly train the dog amounts to over 200 training interludes within a single 3-mile stroll. And each training session is in a different location. You will not believe the improvement within just the first mile of the first walk.

To put it another way, integrating training into a walk offers 200 separate opportunities to use the continuance of the walk as a reward to reinforce the dog's education. Moreover, some training interludes may comprise continuing education for the dog's walking skills: Alternate short periods of the dog walking calmly by your side with periods when the dog is allowed to sniff and investigate the environment. Now sniffing odors on the grass and meeting other dogs become rewards which reinforce the dog's calm and mannerly demeanor. Good Lord! Whatever next? Many enjoyable walks together of course. Happy trails!

THE IMPORTANCE OF TRICKS

Nothing will improve a dog's quality of life better than having a few tricks under her belt. Teaching any trick expands the dog's vocabulary, which facilitates communication and improves the owner's control. Also, specific tricks help prevent and resolve specific behavior problems. For example, by teaching the dog to fetch her toys, the dog learns carrying a toy makes the owner happy and, therefore, will be more likely to chew her toy than other inappropriate items.

More important, teaching tricks prompts owners to lighten up and train with a sunny disposition. Really, tricks should be no different from any other behaviors we put on cue. But they are. When teaching tricks, owners have a much sweeter attitude, which in turn motivates the dog and improves her willingness to comply. The dog feels tricks are a blast, but formal commands are a drag. In fact, tricks are so enjoyable, they may be used as rewards in training by asking the dog to come, sit and down-stay and then rollover for a tummy rub. Go on, try it: Crack a smile and even giggle when the dog promptly and willingly lies down and stays.

Most important, performing tricks prompts onlookers to smile and giggle. Many people are scared of dogs, especially large ones. And nothing can be more off-putting for a dog than to be constantly confronted by strangers who don't like her because of her size or the way she looks. Uneasy people put the dog on edge, causing her to back off and bark, only frightening people all the more. And so a vicious circle develops, with the people's fear fueling the dog's fear *and vice versa*. Instead, tie a pink ribbon to your dog's collar and practice all sorts of tricks on walks and in the park, and you will be pleasantly amazed how it changes people's attitudes toward your friendly dog. The dog's repertoire of tricks is limited only by the trainer's imagination. Below I have described three of my favorites:

SPEAK AND SHUSH

The training sequence involved in teaching a dog to bark on request is no different from that used when training any behavior on cue: request—lure—response—reward. As always, the secret of success lies in finding an effective lure. If the dog always barks at the doorbell, for example, say "Rover, speak!", have an accomplice ring the doorbell, then reward the dog for barking. After a few woofs, ask Rover to "Shush!", waggle a food treat under her nose (to entice her to sniff and thus to shush), praise her when quiet and eventually offer the treat as a reward. Alternate "Speak" and "Shush," progressively increasing the length of shush-time between each barking bout.

PLAY BOW

With the dog standing, say "Bow!" and lower the food lure (palm upwards) to rest between the dog's forepaws. Praise as the dog lowers her forequarters and sternum to the ground (as when teaching the down), but then lure the dog to stand and offer the treat. On successive trials, gradually increase the length of time the dog is required to remain in the play bow posture in order to gain a food reward. If the dog's rear end collapses into a down, say nothing and offer no reward; simply start over.

BE A BEAR

With the dog sitting backed into a corner to prevent her from toppling over backwards, say "Be a bear!" With bent paw and palm down, raise a lure upwards and backwards along the top of the dog's muzzle. Praise the dog when she sits up on her haunches and offer the treat as a reward. To prevent the dog from standing on her hind legs, keep the lure closer to the dog's muzzle. On each trial, progressively increase the length of time the dog is required to sit up to receive a food reward. Since lure-reward training is so easy, teach the dog to stand and walk on her hind legs as well!

Teaching "Be a Bear"

chapter 9

Getting
Active
with your Dog
by Bardi McLennan

Once you and your dog have graduated from basic obedience training and are beginning to work together as a team, you can take part in the growing world of dog activities. There are so many fun things to do with your dog! Just remember, people and dogs don't always learn at the same pace, so don't be upset if you (or your dog) need more than two basic training courses before your team becomes operational. Even smart dogs don't go straight to college from kindergarten!

Just as there are events geared to certain types of dogs, so there are ones that are more appealing to certain types of people. In some

128

activities, you give the commands and your dog does the work (upland game hunting is one example), while in others, such as agility, you'll both get a workout. You may want to aim for prestigious titles to add to your dog's name, or you may want nothing more than the sheer enjoyment of being around other people and their dogs. Passive or active, participation has its own rewards.

Consider your dog's physical capabilities when looking into any of the canine activities. It's easy to see that a Basset Hound is not built for the racetrack, nor would a Chihuahua be the breed of choice for pulling a sled. A loyal dog will attempt almost anything you ask him to do, so it is up to you to know your dog's limitations.

All dogs seem to love playing flyball.

A dog must be physically sound in order to compete at any level in athletic activities, and being mentally sound is a definite plus. Advanced age, however, may not be a deterrent. Many dogs still hunt and herd at ten or twelve years of age. It's entirely possible for dogs to be "fit at 50." Take your dog for a checkup, explain to your vet the type of activity you have in mind and be guided by his or her findings.

You needn't be restricted to breed-specific sports if it's only fun you're after. Certain AKC activities are limited to designated breeds; however, as each new trial, test or sport has grown in popularity, so has the variety of breeds encouraged to participate at a fun level.

But don't shortchange your fun, or that of your dog, by thinking only of the basic function of her breed. Once a dog has learned how to learn, she can be taught to do just about anything as long as the size of the dog is right for the job and you both think it is fun and rewarding. In other words, you are a team.

To get involved in any of the activities detailed in this chapter, look for the names and addresses of the organizations that sponsor them in Chapter 13. You can also ask your breeder or a local dog trainer for contacts.

Official American Kennel Club Activities

The following tests and trials are some of the events sanctioned by the AKC and sponsored by various dog clubs. Your dog's expertise will be rewarded with impressive titles. You can participate just for fun, or be competitive and go for those awards.

OBEDIENCE

Training classes begin with pups as young as three months of age in kindergarten puppy training,

You can compete in obedience trials with a well trained dog.

then advance to pre-novice (all exercises on lead) and go on to novice, which is where you'll start off-lead work. In obedience classes dogs learn to sit, stay, heel and come through a variety of exercises. Once you've got the basics down, you can enter obedience trials and work toward earning your dog's first degree, a C.D. (Companion Dog).

The next level is called "Open," in which jumps and retrieves perk up the dog's interest. Passing grades in competition at this level earn a C.D.X. (Companion Dog Excellent). Beyond that lies the goal of the most ambitious—Utility (U.D. and even U.D.X. or OTCh, an Obedience Champion).

AGILITY

All dogs can participate in the latest canine sport to have gained worldwide popularity for its fun and excitement, agility. It began in England as a canine version of horse show-jumping, but because dogs are more agile and able to perform on verbal commands, extra feats were added such as climbing, balancing and racing through tunnels or in and out of weave poles. Many of the obstacles (regulation or homemade) can be set up in your own backyard. If the agility bug bites, you could end up in international competition!

For starters, your dog should be obedience trained, even though, in the beginning, the lessons may all be taught on lead. Once the dog understands the commands (and you do, too), it's as easy as guiding the dog over a prescribed course, one obstacle at a time. In competition, the race is against the clock, so wear your running shoes! The dog starts with 200 points and the judge deducts for infractions and misadventures along the way.

All dogs seem to love agility and respond to it as if they were being turned loose in a playground paradise. Your dog's enthusiasm will be contagious; agility turns into great fun for dog and owner.

FIELD TRIALS AND HUNTING TESTS

There are field trials and hunting tests for the sporting breeds—retrievers, spaniels and pointing breeds, and for some hounds—Bassets, Beagles and Dachshunds. Field trials are competitive events that test a dog's ability to perform the functions for which she was bred. Hunting tests, which are open to retrievers,

---

TITLES AWARDED BY THE AKC

Conformation: Ch. (Champion)

Obedience: CD (Companion Dog); CDX (Companion Dog Excellent); UD (Utility Dog); UDX (Utility Dog Excellent); OTCh. (Obedience Trial Champion)

Field: JH (Junior Hunter); SH (Senior Hunter); MH (Master Hunter); AFCh. (Amateur Field Champion); FCh. (Field Champion)

Lure Coursing: JC (Junior Courser); SC (Senior Courser)

Herding: HT (Herding Tested); PT (Pre-Trial Tested); HS (Herding Started); HI (Herding Intermediate); HX (Herding Excellent); HCh. (Herding Champion)

Tracking: TD (Tracking Dog); TDX (Tracking Dog Excellent)

Agility: NAD (Novice Agility); OAD (Open Agility); ADX (Agility Excellent); MAX (Master Agility)

Earthdog Tests: JE (Junior Earthdog); SE (Senior Earthdog); ME (Master Earthdog)

Canine Good Citizen: CGC

Combination: DC (Dual Champion—Ch. and Fch.); TC (Triple Champion—Ch., Fch., and OTCh.)

spaniels and pointing breeds only, are noncompetitive and are a means of judging the dog's ability as well as that of the handler.

Hunting is a very large and complex part of canine sports, and if you own one of the breeds that hunts, the events are a great treat for your dog and you. He gets to do what he was bred for, and you get to work with him and watch him do it. You'll be proud of and amazed at what your dog can do.

Fortunately, the AKC publishes a series of booklets on these events, which outline the rules and regulations and include a glossary of the sometimes complicated terms. The AKC also publishes newsletters for field trialers and hunting test enthusiasts. The United Kennel Club (UKC) also has informative materials for the hunter and his dog.

Retrievers and other sporting breeds get to do what they're bred to in hunting tests.

HERDING TESTS AND TRIALS

Herding, like hunting, dates back to the first known uses man made of dogs. The interest in herding today is widespread, and if you own a herding breed, you can join in the activity. Herding dogs are tested for their natural skills to keep a flock of ducks, sheep or cattle together. If your dog shows potential, you can start at the testing level, where your dog can earn a title for showing an inherent herding ability. With training you can advance to the trial level, where your dog should be capable of controlling even difficult livestock in diverse situations.

LURE COURSING

The AKC Tests and Trials for Lure Coursing are open to traditional sighthounds—Greyhounds, Whippets,

Borzoi, Salukis, Afghan Hounds, Ibizan Hounds and Scottish Deerhounds—as well as to Basenjis and Rhodesian Ridgebacks. Hounds are judged on overall ability, follow, speed, agility and endurance. This is possibly the most exciting of the trials for spectators, because the speed and agility of the dogs is awesome to watch as they chase the lure (or "course") in heats of two or three dogs at a time.

TRACKING

Tracking is another activity in which almost any dog can compete because every dog that sniffs the ground when taken outdoors is, in fact, tracking. The hard part comes when the rules as to what, when and where the dog tracks are determined by a person, not the dog! Tracking tests cover a large area of fields, woods and roads. The tracks are laid hours before the dogs go to work on them, and include "tricks" like cross-tracks and sharp turns. If you're interested in search-and-rescue work, this is the place to start.

This tracking dog is hot on the trail.

EARTHDOG TESTS FOR SMALL TERRIERS AND DACHSHUNDS

These tests are open to Australian, Bedlington, Border, Cairn, Dandie Dinmont, Smooth and Wire Fox, Lakeland, Norfolk, Norwich, Scottish, Sealyham, Skye, Welsh and West Highland White Terriers as well as Dachshunds. The dogs need no prior training for this terrier sport. There is a qualifying test on the day of the event, so dog and handler learn the rules on the spot. These tests, or "digs," sometimes end with informal races in the late afternoon.

Here are some of the extracurricular obedience and racing activities that are not regulated by the AKC or UKC, but are generally run by clubs or a group of dog fanciers and are often open to all.

Canine Freestyle This activity is something new on the scene and is variously likened to dancing, dressage or ice skating. It is meant to show the athleticism of the dog, but also requires showmanship on the part of the dog's handler. If you and your dog like to ham it up for friends, you might want to look into freestyle.

Lure coursing lets sighthounds do what they do best—run!

Scent Hurdle Racing Scent hurdle racing is purely a fun activity sponsored by obedience clubs with members forming competing teams. The height of the hurdles is based on the size of the shortest dog on the team. On a signal, one team dog is released on each of two side-by-side courses and must clear every hurdle before picking up its own dumbbell from a platform and returning over the jumps to the handler. As each dog returns, the next on that team is sent. Of course, that is what the dogs are supposed to do. When the dogs improvise (going under or around the hurdles, stealing another dog's dumbbell, and so forth), it no doubt frustrates the handlers, but just adds to the fun for everyone else.

Flyball This type of racing is similar, but after negotiating the four hurdles, the dog comes to a flyball box, steps on a lever that releases a tennis ball into the air, catches the ball and returns over the hurdles to the starting point. This game also becomes extremely fun for spectators because the dogs sometimes cheat by catching a ball released by the dog in the next lane. Three titles can be earned—Flyball Dog (F.D.), Flyball Dog Excellent (F.D.X.) and Flyball Dog Champion (Fb.D.Ch.)—all awarded by the North American Flyball Association, Inc.

Dogsledding The name conjures up the Rocky Mountains or the frigid North, but you can find dogsled clubs in such unlikely spots as Maryland, North Carolina and Virginia! Dogsledding is primarily for the Nordic breeds such as the Alaskan Malamutes, Siberian Huskies and Samoyeds, but other breeds can try. There are some practical backyard applications to this sport, too. With parental supervision, almost any strong dog could pull a child's sled.

Coming over the A-frame on an agility course.

These are just some of the many recreational ways you can get to know and understand your multifaceted dog better and have fun doing it.

chapter 10

Your Dog
and your
Family

by Bardi McLennan

Adding a dog automatically increases your family by one, no matter whether you live alone in an apartment or are part of a mother, father and six kids household. The single-person family is fair game for numerous and varied canine misconceptions as to who is dog and who pays the bills, whereas a dog in a houseful of children will consider himself to be just one of the gang, littermates all. One dog and one child may give a dog reason to believe they are both kids or both dogs.

Either interpretation requires parental supervision and sometimes speedy intervention.

As soon as one paw goes through the door into your home, Rufus (or Rufina) has to make many adjustments to become a part of your family. Your job is to make him fit in as painlessly as possible. An older dog may have some frame of reference from past experience, but to a 10-week-old puppy, everything is brand new: people, furniture, stairs, when and where people eat, sleep or watch TV, his own place and everyone else's space, smells, sounds, outdoors—everything!

Puppies, and newly acquired dogs of any age, do not need what we think of as "freedom." If you leave a new dog or puppy loose in the house, you will almost certainly return to chaotic destruction and the dog will forever after equate your homecoming with a time of punishment to be dreaded. It is unfair to give your dog what amounts to "freedom to get into trouble." Instead, confine him to a crate for brief periods of your absence (up to three or four hours) and, for the long haul, a workday for example, confine him to one untrashable area with his own toys, a bowl of water and a radio left on (low) in another room.

Lots of pets get along with each other just fine.

For the first few days, when not confined, put Rufus on a long leash tied to your wrist or waist. This umbilical cord method enables the dog to learn all about you from your body language and voice, and to learn by his own actions which things in the house are NO! and which ones are rewarded by "Good dog." House-training will be easier with the pup always by your side. Speaking of which, accidents do happen. That goal of "completely housetrained" takes up to a year, or the length of time it takes the pup to mature.

The All-Adult Family

Most dogs in an adults-only household today are likely to be latchkey pets, with no one home all day but the dog. When you return after a tough day on the job, the dog can and should be your relaxation therapy. But going home can instead be a daily frustration.

Separation anxiety is a very common problem for the dog in a working household. It may begin with whines and barks of loneliness, but it will soon escalate into a frenzied destruction derby. That is why it is so important to set aside the time to teach a dog to relax when left alone in his confined area and to understand that he can trust you to return.

Let the dog get used to your work schedule in easy stages. Confine him to one room and go in and out of that room over and over again. Be casual about it. No physical, voice or eye contact. When the pup no longer even notices your comings and goings, leave the house for varying lengths of time, returning to stay home for a few minutes and gradually increasing the time away. This training can take days, but the dog is learning that you haven't left him forever and that he can trust you.

Any time you leave the dog, but especially during this training period, be casual about your departure. No anxiety-building fond farewells. Just "Bye" and go! Remember the "Good dog" when you return to find everything more or less as you left it.

If things are a mess (or even a disaster) when you return, greet the dog, take him outside to eliminate, and then put him in his crate while you clean up. Rant and rave in the shower! *Do not* punish the dog. You were not there when it happened, and the rule is: Only punish as you catch the dog in the act of wrongdoing. Obviously, it makes sense to get your latchkey puppy when you'll have a week or two to spend on these training essentials.

Family weekend activities should include Rufus whenever possible. Depending on the pup's age, now is the time for a long walk in the park, playtime in the backyard, a hike in the woods. Socializing is as important as health care, good food and physical exercise, so visiting Aunt Emma or Uncle Harry and the next-door neighbor's dog or cat is essential to developing an outgoing, friendly temperament in your pet.

If you are a single adult, socializing Rufus at home and away will prevent him from becoming overly protective of you (or just overly attached) and will also prevent such behavioral problems as dominance or fear of strangers.

Babies

Whether already here or on the way, babies figure larger than life in the eyes of a dog. If the dog is there first, let him in on all your baby preparations in the house. When baby arrives, let Rufus sniff any item of clothing that has been on the baby before Junior comes home. Then let Mom greet the dog first before introducing the new family member. Hold the baby down for the dog to see and sniff, but make sure someone's holding the dog on lead in case of any sudden moves. Don't play keep-away or tease the dog with the baby, which only invites undesirable jumping up.

The dog and the baby are "family," and for starters can be treated almost as equals. Things rapidly change, however, especially when baby takes to creeping around on all fours on the dog's turf or, better yet, has yummy pudding all over her face and hands! That's when a lot of things in the dog's and baby's lives become more separate than equal.

Dogs are perfect confidants.

Toddlers make terrible dog owners, but if you can't avoid the combination, use patient discipline (that is, positive teaching rather than punishment), and use time-outs before you run out of patience.

A dog and a baby (or toddler, or an assertive young child) should never be left alone together. Take the dog with you or confine him. With a baby or youngsters in the house, you'll have plenty of use for that wonderful canine safety device called a crate!

Young Children

Any dog in a house with kids will behave pretty much as the kids do, good or bad. But even good dogs and good children can get into trouble when play becomes rowdy and active.

Teach children how to play nicely with a puppy.

Legs bobbing up and down, shrill voices screeching, a ball hurtling overhead, all add up to exuberant frustration for a dog who's just trying to be part of the gang. In a pack of puppies, any legs or toys being chased would be caught by a set of teeth, and all the pups involved would understand that is how the game is played. Kids do not understand this, nor do parents tolerate it. Bring Rufus indoors before you have reason to regret it. This is time-out, not a punishment.

You can explain the situation to the children and tell them they must play quieter games until the puppy learns not to grab them with his mouth. Unfortunately, you can't explain it that easily to the dog. With adult supervision, they will learn how to play together.

Young children love to tease. Sticking their faces or wiggling their hands or fingers in the dog's face is teasing. To another person it might be just annoying, but it is threatening to a dog. There's another difference: We can make the child stop by an explanation, but the only way a dog can stop it is with a warning growl and then with teeth. Teasing is the major cause of children being bitten by their pets. Treat it seriously.

Older Children

The best age for a child to get a first dog is between the ages of 8 and 12. That's when kids are able to accept some real responsibility for their pet. Even so, take the child's vow of "I will never *ever* forget to feed (brush, walk, etc.) the dog" for what it's worth: a child's good intention at that moment. Most kids today have extra lessons, soccer practice, Little League, ballet, and so forth piled on top of school schedules. There will be many times when Mom will have to come to the dog's rescue. "I walked the dog for you so you can set the table for me" is one way to get around a missed appointment without laying on blame or guilt.

Kids in this age group make excellent obedience trainers because they are into the teaching/learning process themselves and they lack the self-consciousness of adults. Attending a dog show is something the whole family can enjoy, and watching Junior Showmanship may catch the eye of the kids. Older children can begin to get involved in many of the recreational activities that were reviewed in the previous chapter. Some of the agility obstacles, for example, can be set up in the backyard as a family project (with an adult making sure all the equipment is safe and secure for the dog).

Older kids are also beginning to look to the future, and may envision themselves as veterinarians or trainers or show dog handlers or writers of the next Lassie best-seller. Dogs are perfect confidants for these dreams. They won't tell a soul.

Other Pets

Introduce all pets tactfully. In a dog/cat situation, hold the dog, not the cat. Let two dogs meet on neutral turf—a stroll in the park or a walk down the street—with both on loose leads to permit all the normal canine ways of saying hello, including routine sniffing, circling, more sniffing, and so on. Small creatures such as hamsters, chinchillas or mice must be kept safe from their natural predators (dogs and cats).

Festive Family Occasions

Parties are great for people, but not necessarily for puppies. Until all the guests have arrived, put the dog in his crate or in a room where he won't be disturbed. A socialized dog can join the fun later as long as he's not underfoot, annoying guests or into the hors d'oeuvres.

There are a few dangers to consider, too. Doors opening and closing can allow a puppy to slip out unnoticed in the confusion, and you'll be organizing a search party instead of playing host or hostess. Party food and buffet service are not for dogs. Let Rufus party in his crate with a nice big dog biscuit.

At Christmas time, not only are tree decorations dangerous and breakable (and perhaps family heirlooms), but extreme caution should be taken with the lights, cords and outlets for the tree lights and any other festive lighting. Occasionally a dog lifts a leg, ignoring the fact that the tree is indoors. To avoid this, use a canine repellent, made for gardens, on the tree. Or keep him out of the tree room unless supervised. And whatever you do, *don't* invite trouble by hanging his toys on the tree!

Car Travel

Before you plan a vacation by car or RV with Rufus, be sure he enjoys car travel. Nothing spoils a holiday quicker than a carsick dog! Work within the dog's comfort level. Get in the car with the dog in his crate or attached to a canine car safety belt and just sit there until he relaxes. That's all. Next time, get in the car, turn on the engine and go nowhere. Just sit. When that is okay, turn on the engine and go around the block. Now you can go for a ride and include a stop where you get out, leaving the dog for a minute or two.

On a warm day, always park in the shade and leave windows open several inches. And return quickly. It only takes 10 minutes for a car to become an overheated steel death trap.

Motel or Pet Motel?

Not all motels or hotels accept pets, but you have a much better choice today than even a few years ago. To find a dog-friendly lodging, look at *On the Road Again With Man's Best Friend*, a series of directories that detail bed and breakfasts, inns, family resorts and other hotels/motels. Some places require a refundable deposit to cover any damage incurred by the dog. More B&Bs accept pets now, but some restrict the size.

If taking Rufus with you is not feasible, check out boarding kennels in your area. Your veterinarian may offer this service, or recommend a kennel or two he or she is familiar with. Go see the facilities for yourself, ask about exercise, diet, housing, and so on. Or, if you'd rather have Rufus stay home, look into bonded petsitters, many of whom will also bring in the mail and water your plants.

chapter 11

Your Dog
and your
Community

by Bardi McLennan

Step outside your home with your dog and you are no longer just family, you are both part of your community. This is when the phrase "responsible pet ownership" takes on serious implications. For starters, it means you pick up after your dog—not just occasionally, but every time your dog eliminates away from home. That means you have joined the Plastic Baggy Brigade! You always have plastic sandwich bags in your pocket and several in the car. It means you teach your kids how to use them, too. If you think this is "yucky," just imagine what

the person (a non-doggy person) who inadvertently steps in the mess thinks!

Your responsibility extends to your neighbors: To their ears (no annoying barking); to their property (their garbage, their lawn, their flower beds, their cat—especially their cat); to their kids (on bikes, at play); to their kids' toys and sports equipment.

There are numerous dog-related laws, ranging from simple dog licensing and leash laws to those holding you liable for any physical injury or property damage done by your dog. These laws are in place to protect everyone in the community, including you and your dog. There are town ordinances and state laws which are by no means the same in all towns or all states. Ignorance of the law won't get you off the hook. The time to find out what the laws are where you live is now.

Be sure your dog's license is current. This is not just a good local ordinance, it can make the difference between finding your lost dog or not. Many states now require proof of rabies vaccination and that the dog has been spayed or neutered before issuing a license. At the same time, keep up the dog's annual immunizations.

Dressing your dog up makes him appealing to strangers.

Never let your dog run loose in the neighborhood. This will not only keep you on the right side of the leash law, it's the outdoor version of the rule about not giving your dog "freedom to get into trouble."

Good Canine Citizen

Sometimes it's hard for a dog's owner to assess whether or not the dog is sufficiently socialized to be accepted by the community at large. Does Rufus or Rufina display good, controlled behavior in public? The AKC's Canine Good Citizen program is available through many dog organizations. If your dog passes the test, the title "CGC" is earned.

The overall purpose is to turn your dog into a good neighbor and to teach you about your responsibility to your community as a dog owner. Here are the ten things your dog must do willingly:

1. Accept a stranger stopping to chat with you.
2. Sit and be petted by a stranger.
3. Allow a stranger to handle him or her as a groomer or veterinarian would.
4. Walk nicely on a loose lead.
5. Walk calmly through a crowd.
6. Sit and down on command, then stay in a sit or down position while you walk away.
7. Come when called.
8. Casually greet another dog.
9. React confidently to distractions.
10. Accept being left alone with someone other than you and not become overly agitated or nervous.

Schools and Dogs

Schools are getting involved with pet ownership on an educational level. It has been proven that children who are kind to animals are humane in their attitude toward other people as adults.

A dog is a child's best friend, and so children are often primary pet owners, if not the primary caregivers. Unfortunately, they are also the ones most often bitten by dogs. This occurs due to a lack of understanding that pets, no matter how sweet, cuddly and loving, are still animals. Schools, along with parents, dog clubs, dog fanciers and the AKC, are working to change all that with video programs for children not only in grade school, but in the nursery school and pre-kindergarten age group. Teaching youngsters how to be responsible dog owners is important community work. When your dog has a CGC, volunteer to take part in an educational classroom event put on by your dog club.

Boy Scout Merit Badge

A Merit Badge for Dog Care can be earned by any Boy Scout ages 11 to 18. The requirements are not easy, but amount to a complete course in responsible dog care and general ownership. Here are just a few of the things a Scout must do to earn that badge:

Point out ten parts of the dog using the correct names.

Give a report (signed by parent or guardian) on your care of the dog (feeding, food used, housing, exercising, grooming and bathing), plus what has been done to keep the dog healthy.

Explain the right way to obedience train a dog, and demonstrate three comments.

Several of the requirements have to do with health care, including first aid, handling a hurt dog, and the dangers of home treatment for a serious ailment.

The final requirement is to know the local laws and ordinances involving dogs.

There are similar programs for Girl Scouts and 4-H members.

Local Clubs

Local dog clubs are no longer in existence just to put on a yearly dog show. Today, they are apt to be the hub of the community's involvement with pets. Dog clubs conduct educational forums with big-name speakers, stage demonstrations of canine talent in a busy mall and take dogs of various breeds to schools for class-room discussion.

The quickest way to feel accepted as a member in a club is to volunteer your services! Offer to help with something—anything—and watch your popularity (and your interest) grow.

Therapy Dogs

Once your dog has earned that essential CGC and reliably demonstrates a steady, calm temperament, you could look into what therapy dogs are doing in your area.

Therapy dogs go with their owners to visit patients at hospitals or nursing homes, generally remaining on leash but able to coax a pat from a stiffened hand, a smile from a blank face, a few words from sealed lips or a hug from someone in need of love.

Nursing homes cover a wide range of patient care. Some specialize in care of the elderly, some in the treatment of specific illnesses, some in physical therapy. Children's facilities also welcome visits from trained therapy dogs for boosting morale in their pediatric patients. Hospice care for the terminally ill and the at-home care of AIDS patients are other areas where this canine visiting is desperately needed. Therapy dog training comes first.

Your dog can make a difference in lots of lives.

There is a lot more involved than just taking your nice friendly pooch to someone's bedside. Doing therapy dog work involves your own emotional stability as well as that of your dog. But once you have met all the requirements for this work, making the rounds once a week or once a month with your therapy dog is possibly the most rewarding of all community activities.

Disaster Aid

This community service is definitely not for everyone, partly because it is time-consuming. The initial training is rigorous, and there can be no let-up in the continuing workouts, because members are on call 24 hours a day to go wherever they are needed at a moment's notice. But if you think you would like to be able to assist in a disaster, look into search-and-rescue work. The network of search-and-rescue volunteers is worldwide, and all members of the American Rescue Dog Association (ARDA) who are qualified to do this work are volunteers who train and maintain their own dogs.

Physical Aid

Most people are familiar with Seeing Eye dogs, which serve as blind people's eyes, but not with all the other work that dogs are trained to do to assist the disabled. Dogs are also specially trained to pull wheelchairs, carry school books, pick up dropped objects, open and close doors. Some also are ears for the deaf. All these assistance-trained dogs, by the way, are allowed anywhere "No Pet" signs exist (as are therapy dogs when

properly identified). Getting started in any of this fascinating work requires a background in dog training and canine behavior, but there are also volunteer jobs ranging from answering the phone to cleaning out kennels to providing a foster home for a puppy. You have only to ask.

Making the rounds with your therapy dog can be very rewarding.

part four

Beyond
the
Basics

chapter 12

Recommended Reading

Books

ABOUT HEALTH CARE

Ackerman, Lowell. *Guide to Skin and Haircoat Problems in Dogs.* Loveland, Colo.: Alpine Publications, 1994.

Alderton, David. *The Dog Care Manual.* Hauppauge, N.Y.: Barron's Educational Series, Inc., 1986.

American Kennel Club. *American Kennel Club Dog Care and Training.* New York: Howell Book House, 1991.

Bamberger, Michelle, DVM. *Help! The Quick Guide to First Aid for Your Dog.* New York: Howell Book House, 1995.

Carlson, Delbert, DVM, and James Giffin, MD. *Dog Owner's Home Veterinary Handbook.* New York: Howell Book House, 1992.

DeBitetto, James, DVM, and Sarah Hodgson. *You & Your Puppy.* New York: Howell Book House, 1995.

Humphries, Jim, DVM. *Dr. Jim's Animal Clinic for Dogs.* New York: Howell Book House, 1994.

McGinnis, Terri. *The Well Dog Book.* New York: Random House, 1991.

Pitcairn, Richard and Susan. *Natural Health for Dogs.* Emmaus, Pa.: Rodale Press, 1982.

ABOUT DOG SHOWS

Hall, Lynn. *Dog Showing for Beginners.* New York: Howell Book House, 1994.

Nichols, Virginia Tuck. *How to Show Your Own Dog.* Neptune, N. J.: TFH, 1970.

Vanacore, Connie. *Dog Showing, An Owner's Guide.* New York: Howell Book House, 1990.

ABOUT TRAINING

Ammen, Amy. *Training in No Time.* New York: Howell Book House, 1995.

Baer, Ted. *Communicating With Your Dog.* Hauppauge, N.Y.: Barron's Educational Series, Inc., 1989.

Benjamin, Carol Lea. *Dog Problems.* New York: Howell Book House, 1989.

Benjamin, Carol Lea. *Dog Training for Kids.* New York: Howell Book House, 1988.

Benjamin, Carol Lea. *Mother Knows Best.* New York: Howell Book House, 1985.

Benjamin, Carol Lea. *Surviving Your Dog's Adolescence.* New York: Howell Book House, 1993.

Bohnenkamp, Gwen. *Manners for the Modern Dog.* San Francisco: Perfect Paws, 1990.

Dibra, Bashkim. *Dog Training by Bash.* New York: Dell, 1992.

Dunbar, Ian, PhD, MRCVS. *Dr. Dunbar's Good Little Dog Book,* James & Kenneth Publishers, 2140 Shattuck Ave. #2406, Berkeley, Calif. 94704. (510) 658–8588. Order from the publisher.

Dunbar, Ian, PhD, MRCVS. *How to Teach a New Dog Old Tricks,* James & Kenneth Publishers. Order from the publisher; address above.

Dunbar, Ian, PhD, MRCVS, and Gwen Bohnenkamp. Booklets on *Preventing Aggression; Housetraining; Chewing; Digging; Barking; Socialization; Fearfulness; and Fighting,* James & Kenneth Publishers. Order from the publisher; address above.

Evans, Job Michael. *People, Pooches and Problems.* New York: Howell Book House, 1991.

Kilcommons, Brian and Sarah Wilson. *Good Owners, Great Dogs.* New York: Warner Books, 1992.

McMains, Joel M. *Dog Logic—Companion Obedience.* New York: Howell Book House, 1992.

Rutherford, Clarice and David H. Neil, MRCVS. *How to Raise a Puppy You Can Live With.* Loveland, Colo.: Alpine Publications, 1982.

Volhard, Jack and Melissa Bartlett. *What All Good Dogs Should Know: The Sensible Way to Train.* New York: Howell Book House, 1991.

ABOUT BREEDING

Harris, Beth J. Finder. *Breeding a Litter, The Complete Book of Prenatal and Postnatal Care.* New York: Howell Book House, 1983.

Holst, Phyllis, DVM. *Canine Reproduction.* Loveland, Colo.: Alpine Publications, 1985.

Walkowicz, Chris and Bonnie Wilcox, DVM. *Successful Dog Breeding, The Complete Handbook of Canine Midwifery*. New York: Howell Book House, 1994.

ABOUT ACTIVITIES

American Rescue Dog Association. *Search and Rescue Dogs*. New York: Howell Book House, 1991.

Barwig, Susan and Stewart Hilliard. *Schutzhund*. New York: Howell Book House, 1991.

Beaman, Arthur S. *Lure Coursing*. New York: Howell Book House, 1994.

Daniels, Julie. *Enjoying Dog Agility—From Backyard to Competition*. New York: Doral Publishing, 1990.

Davis, Kathy Diamond. *Therapy Dogs*. New York: Howell Book House, 1992.

Gallup, Davis Anne. *Running With Man's Best Friend*. Loveland, Colo.: Alpine Publications, 1986.

Habgood, Dawn and Robert. *On the Road Again With Man's Best Friend*. New England, Mid-Atlantic, West Coast and Southeast editions. Selective guides to area bed and breakfasts, inns, hotels and resorts that welcome guests and their dogs. New York: Howell Book House, 1995.

Holland, Vergil S. *Herding Dogs*. New York: Howell Book House, 1994.

LaBelle, Charlene G. *Backpacking With Your Dog*. Loveland, Colo.: Alpine Publications, 1993.

Simmons-Moake, Jane. *Agility Training, The Fun Sport for All Dogs*. New York: Howell Book House, 1991.

Spencer, James B. *Hup! Training Flushing Spaniels the American Way*. New York: Howell Book House, 1992.

Spencer, James B. *Point! Training the All-Seasons Birddog*. New York: Howell Book House, 1995.

Tarrant, Bill. *Training the Hunting Retriever*. New York: Howell Book House, 1991.

Volhard, Jack and Wendy. *The Canine Good Citizen*. New York: Howell Book House, 1994.

General Titles

Haggerty, Captain Arthur J. *How to Get Your Pet Into Show Business*. New York: Howell Book House, 1994.

McLennan, Bardi. *Dogs and Kids, Parenting Tips*. New York: Howell Book House, 1993.

Moran, Patti J. *Pet Sitting for Profit, A Complete Manual for Professional Success*. New York: Howell Book House, 1992.

Scalisi, Danny and Libby Moses. *When Rover Just Won't Do, Over 2,000 Suggestions for Naming Your Dog.* New York: Howell Book House, 1993.

Sife, Wallace, PhD. *The Loss of a Pet.* New York: Howell Book House, 1993.

Wrede, Barbara J. *Civilizing Your Puppy.* Hauppauge, N.Y.: Barron's Educational Series, 1992.

Magazines

The AKC GAZETTE, The Official Journal for the Sport of Purebred Dogs. American Kennel Club, 51 Madison Ave., New York, NY.

Bloodlines Journal. United Kennel Club, 100 E. Kilgore Rd., Kalamazoo, MI.

Dog Fancy. Fancy Publications, 3 Burroughs, Irvine, CA 92718

Dog World. Maclean Hunter Publishing Corp., 29 N. Wacker Dr., Chicago, IL 60606.

Videos

"SIRIUS Puppy Training," by Ian Dunbar, PhD, MRCVS. James & Kenneth Publishers, 2140 Shattuck Ave. #2406, Berkeley, CA 94704. Order from the publisher.

"Training the Companion Dog," from Dr. Dunbar's British TV Series, James & Kenneth Publishers. (See address above).

The American Kennel Club produces videos on every breed of dog, as well as on hunting tests, field trials and other areas of interest to purebred dog owners. For more information, write to AKC/Video Fulfillment, 5580 Centerview Dr., Suite 200, Raleigh, NC 27606.

chapter 13

Resources

Breed Clubs

Every breed recognized by the American Kennel Club has a national (parent) club. National clubs are a great source of information on your breed. You can get the name of the secretary of the club by contacting:

The American Kennel Club
51 Madison Avenue
New York, NY 10010
(212) 696-8200

There are also numerous all-breed, individual breed, obedience, hunting and other special-interest dog clubs across the country. The American Kennel Club can provide you with a geographical list of clubs to find ones in your area. Contact them at the above address.

Registry Organizations

Registry organizations register purebred dogs. The American Kennel Club is the oldest and largest in this country, and currently recognizes over 130 breeds. The United Kennel Club registers some breeds the AKC doesn't (including the American Pit Bull Terrier and the Miniature Fox Terrier) as well as many of the same breeds. The others included here are for your reference; the AKC can provide you with a list of foreign registries.

American Kennel Club
51 Madison Avenue
New York, NY 10010

United Kennel Club (UKC)
100 E. Kilgore Road
Kalamazoo, MI 49001-5598

American Dog Breeders Assn.
P.O. Box 1771
Salt Lake City, UT 84110
(Registers American Pit Bull Terriers)

Canadian Kennel Club
89 Skyway Avenue
Etobicoke, Ontario
Canada M9W 6R4

National Stock Dog Registry
P.O. Box 402
Butler, IN 46721
(Registers working stock dogs)

Orthopedic Foundation for Animals (OFA)
2300 E. Nifong Blvd.
Columbia, MO 65201-3856
(Hip registry)

Activity Clubs

Write to these organizations for information on the
activities they sponsor.

American Kennel Club
51 Madison Avenue
New York, NY 10010
(Conformation Shows, Obedience Trials, Field
Trials and Hunting Tests, Agility, Canine Good

Citizen, Lure Coursing, Herding, Tracking, Earthdog Tests, Coonhunting.)

United Kennel Club
100 E. Kilgore Road
Kalamazoo, MI 49001-5598
(Conformation Shows, Obedience Trials, Agility, Hunting for Various Breeds, Terrier Trials and more.)

North American Flyball Assn.
1342 Jeff St.
Ypsilanti, MI 48198

International Sled Dog Racing Assn.
P.O. Box 446
Norman, ID 83848-0446

North American Working Dog Assn., Inc.
Southeast Kreisgruppe
P.O. Box 833
Brunswick, GA 31521

Trainers

Association of Pet Dog Trainers
P.O. Box 385
Davis, CA 95617
(800) PET–DOGS

American Dog Trainers' Network
161 West 4th St.
New York, NY 10014
(212) 727–7257

National Association of Dog Obedience Instructors
2286 East Steel Rd.
St. Johns, MI 48879

Associations

American Dog Owners Assn.
1654 Columbia Tpk.
Castleton, NY 12033
(Combats anti-dog legislation)

Delta Society
P.O. Box 1080
Renton, WA 98057-1080
(Promotes the human/animal bond through
pet-assisted therapy and other programs)

Dog Writers Assn. of America (DWAA)
Sally Cooper, Secy.
222 Woodchuck Ln.
Harwinton, CT 06791

National Assn. for Search and Rescue (NASAR)
P.O. Box 3709
Fairfax, VA 22038

Therapy Dogs International
6 Hilltop Road
Mendham, NJ 07945